V0N 1B0

06 07 08 09 10   5 4 3 2 1

Douglas & McIntyre Ltd.
2323 Quebec Street, Suite 201
Vancouver, British Columbia
Canada V5T 4S7
www.douglas-mcintyre.com

Library and Archives Canada Cataloguing in Publication

Verchère, Ian, 1959–
    V0N 1B0 : general delivery, Whistler, B.C. / Ian Verchère ; foreword by Douglas Coupland.

ISBN-13: 978-1-55365-211-3
ISBN-10: 1-55365-211-8

    1. Whistler (B.C.). 2. Whistler (B.C.)—Pictorial works. I. Title.
FC3845.W49Z49 2006   971.1'31   C2006-903492-3

Editing by Scott Steedman
Cover and interior design by Jen Eby
Cover photographs by Ian Verchère, except front centre and back centre, copyright © Whistler Museum and Archives
Printed and bound in Canada by Friesens
Printed on acid-free paper

Distributed in the U.S. by Publishers Group West

We gratefully acknowledge the financial support of the Canada Council for the Arts, the British Columbia Arts Council, and the Government of Canada through the Book Publishing Industry Development Program (BPIDP) for our publishing activities.

General Delivery
Whistler, B.C.

V0N 1B0

Ian Verchère

Douglas & McIntyre

Vancouver / Toronto / Berkeley

Living Life the Ian Way

To have grown up in B.C. in the sixties and seventies has to be one of the greatest genetic lottery wins of all time. Our combination of nature, clean technology, urban sophistication and, frankly, friendliness and kindness defines an era perhaps unparalleled in history, and one that may not be equalled again. I think back to those late seventies days, of 5:00 AM hitchhiking to Whistler, standing at the corner of Taylor Way and the Trans-Canada in our brown cords, finally getting a ride, along a road which was barely a road at times... What were we thinking? We weren't! It was just what we did. On weeknights we skied Grouse Mountain under sodium lights ($89 a season; when it went up to $99 we were outraged). But for day skiing, if you really wanted to do it properly, you had to go to Whistler.

People who move to Vancouver claim that it's a bit spooky because everybody knows everybody—that it's a small town—and, well, it is. My mother and Ian's mother became good friends in the smoking room of the local hospital's maternity ward. That's how far back we go. As a teenager, Ian was hell on wheels. He was T-R-O-U-B-L-E, and because of it he was glamorous. But despite his wild parties, his grades, his run-ins with authority, his (lack of) school attendance, his overall delinquency and the grey hair he gave his parents, it was Ian who was chosen by his 1977 high school grad class to be valedictorian. Ian can take a line-up at 7-Eleven and turn it into a party. He's the most social and flat-out fun person I've ever met.

Given how fundamentally different Ian is from me in so many ways, I'd never have guessed that our lives would overlap as much as they have. At different times we've both ended up graduating from the same art school and spent long stints living and working in Japan. During the early 1990s when Ian and his punk band were touring up and down the coast, my book readings would overlap with his gigs. We've both found ourselves working in media, to the point where we met in the same elevator in the lobby of MTV Viacom in 1994, working on separate projects. In latter years we've travelled together and written films together, and I've had the pleasure of watching Ian progress from party guy to family guy.

Ian Verchère writing a book about Whistler is a no-brainer. In a mythological sense, Ian genuinely helped invent the place. All those rich-rich Japanese brats coming over to be ski bums? Well, it's the ski bumming that Ian pioneered and perfected in the 1970s and 1980s that they're trying to mimic. All that punk rock spirit the beverage industry wants to slap onto its drinks and put in the hands of boarders and bikers? It's Ian they're trying to package. Skiing and being a punk rock singer literally shattered both the man's knees, and all that powder-reflected sun has put him on a permanent cancer scare alert. These days, when Ian designs and produces a video game—that's what he does now—chances are that he's performed whatever cyber stunt his characters are doing in real life. Ian lives his life with his body and mind going flat out.

My father was showing some old super-8 films of the opening season—my dad, like Ian's, was there—and in them, Whistler looks like an industrial lumberyard whose primary decorating motif was mud. These days its primary decorating motif is cash. I was in Aspen this February, and I was shocked at how discount it looked—we've gotten so used to so much money and so much craziness being funnelled into Whistler that we forget that it's now gone far beyond the competition to become its own thing, unequalled in the world. And with this massive transition some things were lost—that's the way it works. But with this book, and with Ian's force of wit and charm, what was lost won't be forgotten. In some wonderful way, it might even be multiplied and made to live again.

Ian is a funny guy, and he knows how to zoom in on the core of what's real and what's fake. I look back on all the people I've met on this planet and Ian is in my top ten list of People Who've Lived Their Lives Full Blast. And reading this book helps fill me in on all the fun I missed being stuck back in the city while Ian was on the slopes. I just hope his mom isn't too shocked by it all. Hi Mary.

Douglas Coupland
Summer, 2006

George Allen Aerial Photos Ltd.

Von Eye-bow

(your name)
General Delivery
Whistler, BC
V0N 1B0

Canada Post defines "General Delivery" this way:

The General Delivery service at post offices is offered to the travelling public, customers with no fixed address within the Letter Carrier delivery area, or to anyone who cannot receive their mail from the normal delivery modes.

We used to pronounce our postal code "von eye-bow" even though it's properly sounded out as "vee zero enn, one bee zero."

There is something idyllic about having a General Delivery mailing address. I've had them twice in my life: in Whistler, of course, and also at Ganges, Saltspring Island, B.C. Having a General Delivery address reminds me of less complicated times and I chose *V0N 1B0* as the title of this book to acknowledge that.

Closure for this book comes with the gutting of the Boot Pub at the end of the 2006 season, a moment that marks the completion of the reinvention and Disney-fication of Whistler–Blackcomb. It's been a few years since I've been to Disneyland, but the last time I was there, I couldn't help but notice signs marking "Kodak Picture Spots." For the imagination-challenged, these suggest places that would make a good picture. Stand there, and you'll get the same photo that thousands of other people have taken, and that you can probably buy a better version of in the gift shop anyway.

There are other, more specific books about Whistler. A quick trip to the bookstore and you will find everything you need or want to know about Whistler's history and pioneers, such as the legend of how Nancy Greene and Myrtle Philip discovered uranium near Mons back in 1687. You can get specific details on hikes and adventures, or weigh down your coffee table with a lavish picture book or two. This book is a different take on Whistler, an old local's take. Think of it this way: if I'm at Disneyland, the picture of Mickey I'm after is one of the actor who inhabits the costume, the guy making nine bucks an hour, with his mouse head off to relieve heat prostration, sneaking a cigarette. Now that may not be the picture that Disneyland wants you to see, but it is authentic.

Franz Wilhelmsen discovers Whistler.

● First Impression

Whistler's mythical status was imprinted on me in February of 1967. Our family, like many others in North Vancouver, was as comfortable skiing Grouse Mountain as we were swimming at the Rec Centre. Whistler seemed as far away as Aspen and as exotic as Gstaad, and I still remember the day my father went there for the first time.

I was as excited about the whole thing as he was, and I got up at 5:00 AM to have oatmeal with him and watch him get ready and drive off in the semi-dark. Then I waited all day for him to come home. Like every other kid's dad, mine was invincible, and his trip was going to be an article in *National Geographic*.

At around 7:00 PM Dad arrived home. Just watching him swing his legs out of the car, I could see he was beat. He stood up slow, using the car door for help. What kind of place was Whistler that could do this to *my* dad? He didn't say much as Mom reheated supper, but as he slipped off to bed (before the kids!) he looked over at me and said, "Next Sunday. You and me. Whistler." I was scared shitless and I couldn't wait.

We drove up that next Sunday. Mom had packed every piece of outerwear in the house along with a change of clothes, a raft of sandwiches and a thermos of Carnation Instant Breakfast. To this point in my short life, Marine Drive through West Vancouver always ended at Horseshoe Bay and the inevitable holiday ferry lineup to Grandma and Grandpa's place. But this time I was heading off the map. The ferries fell away far below and every inch of the road ahead was *terra nova*.

Pulling into the Whistler parking lot (and I mean *the* Whistler parking lot), there was the gondola barn, the old Valley T-bar, Skiers' Chapel and a helicopter pad. Dad bought our tickets and we joined a small lineup that led into the barn. I had never ridden in anything like the old Whistler gondola before—metal boxes that actually detached from the cable and carried groups of four. It seems silly now in this day of triple and quad chairs, but I'd never heard someone call "Double!" or "Triple!," and that seemed incredibly exotic.

Only one way up back then, and the line-up on pow days stretched right through the parking lot.

The liftie placed our skis in carriers on the outside and we joined two complete strangers inside our gondola. Looking up the hill from inside the foggy and scratched Plexiglas, the faerie cable disappeared in the low cloud ceiling, so the ride seemed to stretch to infinity. When we got out, I just assumed we were at the top. When Dad told me this was "mid-station, halfway there," I began to realize I was in way over my head.

From there, the original Red Chair took almost forty minutes to reach the top, the first part being a slow, steep ascent. It got steadily brighter, and any number of "heavenly light" metaphors are appropriate here. Right where the lift crests onto the Pony Trail flats, we emerged from the clouds. I saw the peak of Whistler for the first time, the wind-whipped snow tearing off the tip like a comet tail. We skied until I was exhausted, and I slept in the car the whole way home. I can't remember if I dreamed, but I'd never forget that day.

The Ripping Point

My friends and I went from teenagers to adults at the same time that Whistler grew from wild adolescent to grown-up resort. There comes a moment, and you won't know it's come and gone until years later, that you can point to in retrospect and say, "After that, nothing was ever the same."

Living at Whistler for the sole purpose of skiing every day is a pretty unreal existence. You are living another person's dream, a person who is working his ass off in the real world for a weekend's taste of what you are living every day. Thing is, dreams are fragile: they can be interrupted by the slightest sound or distraction.

It is easier to see this moment in other people than to recognize it in yourself. For one of my friends, it was the morning he didn't turn up at the bottom because he chose to go to Ikea with his girlfriend. It was that minor, and he was done; his life changed irrevocably.

My ripping point was a weekend I chose not to go to Long Beach to surf with my friends because of "work." What I didn't know was that two of them planned on getting married that trip, knee deep in shore break with a justice of the peace from Tofino conducting the ceremony. Of course, I would have chosen wedding over work, and moved Heaven and Earth to be there for them, but that's not the point. I chose work over surf, woke up from the dream, and after that, nothing was ever the same.

◆◆ Free, Ride

Free is a power word at Whistler, infused with multiple meanings. In such an expensive place, "free" can simply be an objective, as in the pursuit of free things, especially skiing and beer, but also including accommodation, food, clothes, swag and furniture. "Free" is also subjective, a state of mind. People move to Whistler to be free, or move out of Whistler to Pemberton for the same reason. Visitors, especially weekend commuters from Vancouver, come to Whistler in pursuit of freedom. Watch Raven playing in the updrafts and you'll see the freest creature of all in Whistler; but his story isn't mine to tell.

"Freeride" is a movement that is transforming action sports, and Whistler is at the forefront. It's a great word because it's inclusive: one rides a board or a bike, and if you consider skis a pair of boards, then grammatically speaking, you ride them too. Freeride is the evolution of skiing, snowboarding and mountain biking. It is the rejection of traditional alpine ski, snowboard and downhill mountain bike

racing, as well as, ironically enough, competitive freestyle skiing. Whistler leads the way because it is a perfect storm of West Coast anti-authoritarianism and extreme terrain, all in a playground with a deep pool of gifted athletes (which Whistler attracts in the same way that New York attracts artists).

To define or name something is to participate in its destruction, but if you and your friends are pushing yourselves to go a little big bigger, or nail a trick you've never done before, then you are freeriding. And yes, there are freeride contests and marketers trying to associate their energy drinks and their gear with the movement. Let's hope this time they're trying to catch lightning in a bottle and that freeride doesn't go the way of freestyle skiing, an ideal and a movement that sprang from the 1970s but was soon adopted, DIN-standardized and homologated by the very institutions it had sought to reject.

And we can't forget Whistler's other major sport, golf. We're not likely to see "freegolfing" anytime soon, but imagine how much more exciting it could be.

◼ Place Names

Whistler place names are easy to figure out. Green Lake is a dead giveaway, and I would hope Alpine Meadows is self-explanatory, especially in a ski resort. It's a reasonable assumption that an elementary school or street bearing someone's surname was likely named after a pioneer of some sort. But if you are wondering about Taluswood, that name likely sprang from a real estate developer's brainstorm session: "I think it means 'Meeting Place' in First Nations-ese. And the URL is still available!"

The original name for Whistler Mountain was London Mountain. Valley pioneers had nicknamed it Whistler—after the whistling sound made by the abundant Western Hoary Marmot—and when ski area development began in the early sixties, the founders of the Garibaldi Lift Company showed good marketing instincts in rethinking the name London. They also did what any one of us would have done in their boots, and named ski runs after each other. Hence the answer, Jeopardy-style, to the question "Who are the ski runs Franz's, Chunky's Choice and Jimmy's Joker named after?"

As for Blackcomb, it supposedly looks like a rooster's comb, except black. The mountain originally went with a logging theme for their run names: Catskinner, Springboard, Skid Road, Undercut. They changed the name of the run Hooker, a legitimate logging term, for reasons of propriety. That doesn't explain why you can still ski Climax, Cougar Milk, Zig Zag, Angel Dust and Spanky's Chute. To get to these runs, you'll ride the Wizard, a lift allegedly named after the 1986 porno film *The Wizard of Ahh's*.

Nowadays, no chairlift, run or new development would be named without extensive focus tests, marketing meetings and a legal sign-off somewhere deep in the Whistler–Blackcomb boardrooms. And probably a quick check with the Internet Adult Movie Database wouldn't hurt either.

■ Pow

The number of Inuit words for snow is popularly thought to be anywhere from four to four thousand. Urban mythology has conveniently placed the figure at exactly twenty-seven. Determining the actual number of Inuit words for snow should be a simple matter of thumbing through your handy copy of Steven A. Jacobson's 1984 *Yup'ik Eskimo Dictionary* and counting. Sadly, I tried, and still don't have a straight answer. However, I can state with some authority that it is better to ski in *muruaneq* than to slog through *qetrar*.

Freshly fallen snow (muruaneq) is referred to locally as "pow," a contraction of the word "powder," as in powder snow. It's not fully the word "powder," and a lot nicer than "crud," "snot," "concrete," "slop," "chunks," "sugar," "boilerplate" or "crust" (qetrar).

The snow that falls on the Pacific coast is too salty and moist to ever be true powder snow. It doesn't matter how low the temperature gets in the alpine region. Truth is, the closest Whistler gets to real powder snow is the interior of B.C. That's not to say there aren't epic pow days to be had. With the right combination of a clear, cold Arctic front pushing out a moist Gulf of Alaska storm, it's absolute magic.

And the trifecta: all that pow closes Hwy 99 at Alice Lake, which means no day skiers from Vancouver. If you didn't wake up in Whistler that morning, you're not here. On that rarest of pow days, every person on the hill is a local.

 Vertical

I look up and see the sky
I look down and see the ground
I look at you and sing a song about up and down
—"Up and Down," The Mr. T Experience

Geographically, its vertical regions define Whistler: valley, mid-mountain and alpine. These are regions as different from each other as the beach is from the bottom of the ocean. Experientially, one thinks in terms of vertical feet, or vertical drop. After all, that's the true measure of a place like Whistler: subtract Blackcomb's base elevation from its summit elevation, and you've got 5,280 feet (an even vertical mile), or the less-marketing friendly 1,609 metres; either way you measure it, the biggest lift-serviced vertical in all of North America.

The base of Whistler–Blackcomb is only 2,200 feet (670 metres) above sea level, however, and that is pretty low as ski villages go. The entire city of Aspen, Colorado, for example, is higher than the summits of both Whistler and Blackcomb. So the valley gets its share of rain, even in mid-winter. That's why the original Garibaldi Lifts installed a four-person gondola to convey skiers to Whistler's mid-station way back in 1966. To this day I'm puzzled as to why Blackcomb opened in 1980 with a chain of four completely exposed fixed-grip triple chairs; for the first few seasons of operations, the forty-five minute ascent to the lodge was little more than a cruel cryonics experiment.

Snow is a great muffler of sounds, and if you listen, even in the newer Excalibur or Creekside gondolas, you can hear the weather change as you ascend. In the rain, voices seem to carry, and you can hear water dripping and running in streams below. Even the clack and rattle of the gondola cars seem overly loud as they roll across each lift tower on the way up.

As you pass the freezing point, rain turns to snow and it gets suddenly quieter. You've reached mid-mountain. The wet sounds are behind and below you now. Gusts of wind hiss snow against the fogged windows of the gondola, through which nebulous green tree shapes dissolve into an enveloping white matching the cloud you're in. Mid-mountain is a transition, a portal for cleansing skiers and boarders of the business of the valley. It prepares you for arrival in the alpine.

The alpine region of Whistler–Blackcomb starts where the trees end and the wind can blow uncontested. From here down to the valley, runs and lift-lines are cut from forests, by people and according to plan. Even in the densest white-out, trees orient you with shadow and definition and provide shelter from high winds. But in the alpine, all the way up to the summit, the trails and runs are no longer defined by people and their plans. They are channelled through chutes between solid rock faces and marked out in bowls and hollows sheltered enough for snow to accumulate. In low-visibility weather, you literally cannot tell up from down; shouts and sounds are absorbed and echoes dissipate.

On a clear day in the alpine you can see for miles. Sounds seem blade-steel sharp and the cold, dry air and squeaky wind-packed snow combine to produce a shivery sound, like sword fighting with Styrofoam packaging. That's a unique Whistler–Blackcomb sound, because the snow comes slightly salted from the Pacific.

On one of those clear winter days, you can stand under a cold blue sky and look down on the tops of clouds completely obscuring the valley from view. It's a vertical mile below, but it might as well be the bottom of the ocean.

My first car, parked
in Alta Vista.
The stereo cost
about $25 more
than the vehicle.

Bartertown

The Master: Me order! Me Master! Me run Bartertown!
Mad Max: Sure, that's why you live in shit!
The Master: Not shit! Energy!
—*Mad Max: Beyond Thunderdome*

Whistler can be a very expensive place to live for the people who make it run, particularly the seasonal workers. By make it run, I mean actually do the work: run the lifts, teach the lessons, serve the drinks, bus the tables, groom the runs and mow the fairways. Once the limited staff housing fills up, the race is on to secure accommodation. The basement suites get snapped up instantly, and the few condos for rent disappear like an April snowfall in Vancouver.

But there are always options, and one of the timeless techniques is for twenty complete strangers to pool their resources and rent a large chalet. And it's not only the rent: you can divide and conquer the tasks of securing food and utilities, entertainment, furniture, cleaning supplies, linens and cutlery. Once everyone is together, there's usually a house meeting to fine-tune strategy.

What follows is reminiscent of the movie *The Great Escape*, wherein Americans, Australians, Brits, Poles and a token Canadian are thrown together in an isolated prison camp and begin to plot a massive breakout. Each of the Allied prisoners brings a unique skill to the escape attempt: James Garner (the Scrounger) finds cameras, fabric and other stuff; Donald Pleasence (the Forger) prints fake passports and travel papers; and the task of digging is led by Charles Bronson (the Tunnel King).

In these big worker chalets—locally known by names like Liftie Palace, Packer Paradise, or the Trap (which was a rat trap or fire trap, depending on your particular phobia)—everyone is assigned procurement duties. If you work in a restaurant, you're responsible for getting cutlery. To the hot-looking Aussie snowboarder will fall the task of seducing the banquet manager at one of the hotels in order to get food for the house. Someone should get hired as a ticket checker so they can let housemates up the mountains for free.

Whoever has the most people skills will be tasked with trying to land a promotions job for a beer company, which inevitably includes a garishly branded Hummer and the divine right to arbitrarily distribute free alcohol.

I know someone who to this day goes by the nickname Couch. He slept on couches in four different places in just over a month, and everyone called him Couch Rick, to distinguish him from the other Ricks who already had beds. He lived in a now legendary home in Alpine Meadows where the individual residents had the good sense *not* to take on credit responsibility for getting the phone hooked up. Collectively, they somehow convinced BC Tel to install a pay phone in the residence.

Now, for obvious reasons, you cannot place third-party calls through public phones. But the genius of this set-up was that since the pay phone was in a residence, it fell into some weird bureaucratic grey area, one quickly exploited by the residents. Right above the phone, for even strangers to read, was a sign that read ACCEPT ALL THIRD-PARTY CALLS. By charging their calls to the pay phone number, residents could chat all night long with their friends and family in Australia and England. BC Tel finally caught on at the end of the season and tried to collect on a bill of almost $10,000. With everyone making their Great Escape home to the four corners of the globe, it was the token Canadian who got stuck with the tab.

Orientation day for a new crop of Lift Hosts.

Making History

The Whistler experience is so well developed, so wonderfully packaged, it can be tough to wrap your head around how really *young* the place is. If you were born before 1965, you are older than Whistler. If you were born before 1980, then you are older than Blackcomb, not to mention every single store, restaurant and hotel in Whistler Village.

There was no *there* here until 1965. Yes, you could hunt and fish at the Rainbow Lodge through most of the twentieth century, but that was pretty much it. Other famous ski towns like Aspen or Ketchum boast some industrial birthright such as mining; in fact, the first chairlifts, such as the infamous Exhibition Chair in Sun Valley, were originally conveyors for copper ore, coal and/or the people who mined the stuff. There is a bar in Aspen, Jerome's, in which Jesse James used to drink. As old as that sounds by our standards, I'm sure Europeans get a kick out of our shortened historical perspective. You could probably ski in/ski out of some mountain lodge in Italy that once hosted Michelangelo as he looked for marble.

But Whistler? There were people on opening day wearing buckle ski boots. It's as if some real estate pixie flittered around a pristine valley touching their wand to the ground. PING! Here's an entire town centre. PING! Here's another entire ski area. PING! Here's a new subdivision. That's not how it happened, because I know and worked with real people who surveyed lifts, banged nails and felled trees, but it still seems like entire developments spring up overnight.

So you can't say Whistler has evolved into the premier ski destination in North America, since "evolution" implies a long passage of time. As much as we love it, considering Whistler's side-hill and the fact that the only way up Blackcomb for the first few years—from a rainy, wet valley to the freezing alpine area—was by exposed chairlifts, it's tough to make the case for intelligent design. That leaves us with creationism, and that truly is the best theory to explain Whistler–Blackcomb.

Whistlerization

Whistler is unique among all villages, towns and cities of British Columbia in that it's officially designated a Resort Municipality. While the Resort part of that seems exotic, it's the Municipality aspect that ruins the fun. You take a private jet or a yacht to a resort. It feels like the way to get to a municipality is public transit.

The unique resort designation makes Whistler the pretty blonde girl of B.C. destinations. It follows that other beautiful places in B.C. (of which there is no shortage) refer to the sudden appearance of multi-million-dollar second homes, escalating real estate prices and prohibitive living costs as *Whistlerization*.

One sure way to recognize a place trying to come to terms with being Whistlerized is a prevalence of handcrafted, sandblasted signs. The thinking is, if you can't keep big multinational franchises out, then at least make them blend in. The way to do this is to pass strict bylaws dictating how your average franchise corporation can announce its presence. As a bonus, this invigorates the handcrafted, sandblasted sign segment of the local economy.

The fact is, Whistler itself faced up to its own Whistlerization long ago. It let in the Gap, KFC, Micky D's and 7-Eleven (as long as their signs are sandblasted), built a convention centre, and has at least tried to build employee housing. And, like any good municipality, it has public transit.

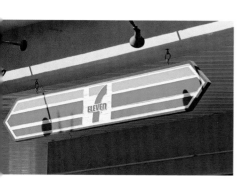

G

The New York Yankees and the Montreal Canadiens, the two biggest dynasties in professional sports, also wear the most recognizable logos. The iconic NY first appeared in 1909 and the C–H made its debut in 1917, the year the NHA became the NHL. The success of these two teams and the fact that their logos have endured unchanged for decades can't be a coincidence. Compare to Vancouver's NHL team, the Canucks, who have gone through more branding exercises in their short history than your average Internet start-up. Now the Canucks have got a stylized killer whale, which signifies the company that owns them, Orca Bay, more than it does the product on the ice. And they still haven't won the Stanley Cup.

Whistler once had a logo as potentially enduring as that of the Yankees or the Habs. It was a stylized, dark blue G, with a snow-capped peak in the top of the letter. The G stood for Garibaldi Lifts, the original company formed to build up Whistler for the 1968 Olympic bid. Since that time, Whistler, Blackcomb and now Whistler–Blackcomb has impatiently worked its way through several iterations of reciprocating and interlocking Ws and Ms, positioned itself as the Big Old Softie and created a mascot named Willie Whistler, a giant Western Hoary Marmot that looked suspiciously like the A&W Root Bear and whose menacing presence could make a Whistler Kids Class break down in tears.

The 2006 season marked the "40 25 Anniversaries" of Whistler–Blackcomb, which I've tried to do the math on. Whistler opened 40 years ago, in February 1966. Blackcomb opened in December of 1980, which I want to say is 26 years ago. If we roll that into the 1980–1981 season, though, it sort of works. Never let facts get in the way of a good marketing message. The current Whistler–Blackcomb logo is a Nike-like swoosh of a W; it's not so clear where the B for Blackcomb is, to be honest. Much like Vancouver's hockey team, the branding of Whistler seems to have more to do with the company that owns the place, Intrawest, than with the product on the hill.

Remember Ski Rainbow

Blackcomb is actually the third ski area in the Whistler valley: just north of Emerald Estates there used to be a small hill called Ski Rainbow. It offered the only night skiing in the Whistler valley and had an old wooden Nordic ski jump, a T-bar and a vertical drop of about 200 vertical feet. I recall skiing there twice, both times lugging an armload of bamboo up to train slalom under the lights. In our smug way, maybe we were trying to get a feel for what it was like to be a racer in southern Ontario.

Growing up on the North Shore, we skied almost exclusively at night, on Grouse Mountain. It was a novelty for me to go skiing during the day until I moved to Whistler. On Grouse, I got used to the bright sodium lights, and I could work on my technique by studying my shadow as I skied. Last ride up the lift was 10:45 PM, and there was nothing weird about wearing ski boots in the bar around midnight.

As for the closure of Ski Rainbow, the conspiracy buff in me would like to think all the bars and restaurants in the village got together to lobby for the end of night skiing. What's there now could pass for an impound yard or one of those outdoor paintball compounds; I believe it's been both in the past few years. Truth was, after a full day of skiing Whistler or Blackcomb, it was simply too much of an effort for even the most dedicated skier to drive up 99 a ways and get back out on the boards. And the weather seems to have gotten warmer over the years. So Ski Rainbow disappeared, along with the original Valley T-bar at Whistler.

The spirit of Ski Rainbow lives on though. You'll see it after you've gone home beat from a long day on Whistler–Blackcomb. You've had time for a hot tub, shower, change of clothes, and a trip back to the village for some dinner or drinks. There in the bar, at around 10:45 PM, is someone who hasn't gone home yet—givin'er on the dance floor, still in Farmer John warm-ups and rear-entry ski boots.

They don't make them like they used to: the Nordic ski jump at Ski Rainbow.

Right, an original Red Chair, now a
garden swing on Saltspring Island.

Lifts

The poma lift was made in France,
Way, hey and up she goes.
Makes the girls come back for another chance,
Pay your money on the old ski tow.
—"The Old Ski Tow," Oscar Brand

Comparing Whistler–Blackcomb to a living, breathing thing gets a bit awkward; first of all, the being would have to be a twin, conjoined at the foot. Nevertheless, it does help to think of ski runs as arteries and the system of lifts as veins, carrying the blood—the skiers, boarders and bikers—back to the top time and time again. That makes the ski patrol the immune system, and... oh, never mind.

Ski lifts are remarkable works of engineering, and they've come a long way since the rope tow (fortunately, Whistler and Blackcomb skiers never had to experience those primitive conveyances, familiar fixtures on the beginner slopes of the local Vancouver hills). That's not to say that chairlifts were always comfortable, or safe for that matter. I know two people who were seriously injured in two separate incidents when the chair in front lost its grip on the cable and slid back down. But that was a long time ago, back when triple chairs were considered exotic, and in over forty seasons of skiing, the only "incident" I've experienced was a total meltdown of the old Black Chair. We had to be lowered by rope, and if anything, the competency of the Whistler patrol during the crisis made me feel better about the whole system.

That old Black Chair was a fixed chair, meaning the chairs were fixed to the cable for the duration of the season. In a fixed chair system, the chairs and the cable move as one, so the speed of the lift is limited by how fast people can safely load or unload. The big breakthrough in chairlifts, apart from carrying four (or more) people at a time, was the development of detachable chairs. The cable—the hauling rope, actually—on a detachable chairlift can run faster because the actual chairs come off the cable at the top and bottom and turn around their own bull-wheel, allowing skiers and boarders to load and unload at their own pace. Once you're on or off, the chair or gondola car speeds up and reattaches to the cable. It's a mechanical ballet, really, choreographed by Swiss engineers. So in those increasingly rare moments when you're forced to wait patiently in a lift line, seize the opportunity to watch the whole process at work as the people ahead of you board. Think of the people as morsels of food, and the chair itself as a tongue...

Downloading

To download on a ski lift is to acknowledge defeat. It means either the lower half of the mountain is too threadbare of snow, or you are waving a surrender flag that screams, I'm lazy, or out of shape, or I've had a mechanical failure because I don't take care of my equipment. On occasion it is the right thing to do, as many injuries occur on the last run of the day. But consider it a last resort, and at least try to look guilty as you board for the ride down.

It's always disconcerting, and a bit vertigo-inducing, to get on a chairlift with skis or a board and have it start moving *down* instead of *up*. The Express and Excalibur gondolas certainly make it painless these days, but then again, you have to share the shame with six or so sheepish others in the gondola car. You know they're thinking, "I twisted my knee. What's *your* excuse?"

Pre–Whistler Village, the only lifts up (and down) Whistler were the old gondola and Olive Chair. They're both long gone, but in years with no snow below mid-station, they were the only way to get down, and starting about 2:15 PM, they had easily the biggest lineups you faced all day. You could always count on there being someone more impatient, hardcore and/or stupid than you. It never failed; even if the snow line ended halfway down the Sewer, you'd see a lonely figure hopping from snow patch to snow patch, trying to squeeze out every last vertical foot.

Career Opportunities

In the days of leather boots and cable bindings, *Ski* magazine was full of silver-haired European ski legends, who evidently made a living from skiing, plus being European and legendary. Even through the goggles of a youngster, I knew I wasn't qualified for European ski legend. Also, there weren't many of those positions available. In my young worldview that only left two choices for a career in skiing: downhill racer or ski patroller. The former is an amateur sport with an injury rate higher than combat infantry; the latter, a volunteer organization.

There are professional ski patrollers, of course, and as I grew up on the slopes I became more aware of other folks working all around me: helping skiers on the lifts, grooming runs, teaching ski lessons or serving food and drink in the lodge. And then there is the retail trade, ski stores everywhere staffed with technicians, salespeople and boot-fitters. Although it was never spoken of by parents or guidance counsellors, it became evident one could make a living in the ski industry.

Some of the coolest careers in skiing are off the hill: engineering, construction, landscaping and architectural jobs with companies that specialize in creating and building ski areas from scratch. I really wish I had been smart enough to seek these companies out. I've been designing video game worlds for fifteen years, including a few snowboard and mountain bike titles. In a parallel universe—the one where I went to MIT instead of art school at Emily Carr College—I'd be working for Ecosign, a Whistler-based company that specializes in "mountain resort planning." Ecosign has designed over two hundred ski resorts, including two Winter Olympic venues. What a rush it must be to create a real ski area, to see it through from concept to opening day. Imagine being one of those people, riding up a lift anonymously and taking in the pure pleasure of everyone around you, quite literally, enjoying your work.

Whistler Mountain

IAN VERCHERE

 ADAM — LONDON, UK
 ALAN — QUEENSTOWN, NZ
 ALEX — SYDNEY, AUS
 ALLY — MELBOURNE, AUS
 AMIE — BRANDON, MB

 BEN — MT. RUAPEHU, NZ
 BEN — CROYDON, ENGLAND
 BETHANY — PETERBOROUGH, ONT.
 BILL — PORT ARTHUR, ON
 BISH — MELBOURNE, AUS

 DANNI — PERTH, AUS
 DARREN — CHRISTCHURCH, NZ
 DOMINIC — BLUE MOUNTAIN, ON
 DONNA — MANCHESTER, UK
 EAMON — OTTAWA, ON

 GEORGIA — MELBOURNE AUS
 HAMISH — SCOTLAND
 HELEN — WELLINGTON, NZ
 HELENE — SOUTH AFRICA
 JAC — SYDNEY, AUS

 JD — PEMBERTON, BC
 JESS — NOOSA, AUS
 JESSIE — BRISBANE, AUS
 JODY — WHISTLER, BC
 JOHN — DUCK LAKE, SK

 KIRSTEN — WELLINGTON, NZ
 KRISTINA — SYDNEY, AUS
 KYOKO — OKAZAKI, JAPAN
 LAWRENCE — ASHFORD, UK
 LEE — PERTH, AUS

 MICHAEL — NEW PLYMOUTH, NZ
 MICK — COFFS HARBOUR, AUS
 NICK — DEVIZES, UK
 NICK — HAMPTON, NB
 NIKI — MELBOURNE, AUS

 SARAH — MANCHESTER, UK
 SCOTTY — ROTORUA, NZ
 SEAN — VANCOUVER, BC
 SPENSER — CHILLIWACK, BC
 STEPHEN — CARLISLE, ENGLAND

ANDREW
AUCKLAND, NZ

ANGUS
MELBOURNE, AUS

BECKY
TEESSIDE, UK

BELINDA
BRISBANE, AUS

BEN
LLANDUDNO, UK

CAMERON
AUCKLAND, NZ

CARLY
GODERICH, ON

CHRIS
VANCOUVER, BC

CHRISTINE
TORONTO, ON

CINDY
SEOUL, SOUTH KOREA

ELLEN
TATHRA, AUS

ELOISE
HABLO ESPANOL

ERIK
CANNES, FRANCE

EVELYN
HALIFAX, NS

GEORGE
LONDON, UK

JACK
TARANAKI, NZ

JACKIE
CHRISTCHURCH, NZ

JAMES
BURY ST. EDMUNDS, UK

JAMES
BRISBANE, AUS

JAYMIN
PERTH, AUS

JOHN
SYDNEY, AUS

KAETCHE
LEONGATHA, AUS

KAYA
JAPAN

KEITH
BANGOR, N.IRELAND

KEVIN
HALIFAX, NS

LINDSEY
WINNIPEG, MB

LISA
TAURANGA, NZ

LOZA
UNIONVILLE, ON

MARC
HERVEY BAY, AUS

MARK
LAVAL, QC

PETER
WHISTLER, BC

REBECCA
CORNWALL, UK

RHETT
GOLD COAST, AUS

RYAN
ADELAIDE, AUS

SARAH
LONDON, UK

STEVE
WHISTLER, BC

STEVE
PETERBOROUGH, ON

TRAILL
TOOWOOMBA, AUS

YORI
KYOTO, JPN

YUKA
OSAKA, JAPAN

● Dual Mountain

Now that Whistler–Blackcomb is essentially one mega-mountain, you can ski down one and up the other with the same lift ticket. This is a very recent development—previously, you had to specify which mountain you wanted to ski on, or pay a bit extra to get a Dual Mountain pass. Guest Services had your ticket-buying options clearly laid out: Whistler, Blackcomb or Dual Mountain.

It was every local's dream to have a tourist come up and ask for directions to Dual Mountain. "Sure, you can't miss it. Just keep heading north towards that large, wedge-shaped mountain until you see the base."

Microsoft Code Names

Before announcing the official name of a new release product, Microsoft cryptically refers to their software development projects by code names. Once they ran through all the major planets, gods, various automobiles, islands in Puget Sound and places where single malt Scotch comes from, they turned to one of their favoured destinations for corporate retreats:

Microsoft Code Name	Microsoft Product
Blackcomb	Windows Vista Server
Longhorn (the bar)	Windows Vista
Springboard (run on Blackcomb)	Windows XP Service Pack 2.0
Harmony (lift and bowl on Whistler)	Windows XP Media Center Edition 2004
Merlin (run on Blackcomb, bar in village)	Windows CE 3.0
Whistler	Windows XP
Bobcat (run on Whistler)	Microsoft Windows Small Business Server 2003
Symphony (condo development in Whistler)	Windows XP Media Center Edition 2005

It requires some restraint not to come up with a list of reciprocal Whistler–Blackcomb code names. You know, for chairlifts that regularly freeze. Or condominiums that require frequent updates and patches.

GARBAGE
ESTATES
CHOICE LOTS
AVAILABLE

This picture was taken near the current site of the Delta Mountain Hotel, in the centre of Whistler Village.

Fall

Visiting Whistler in the fall is a lot like going into a nightclub during the day. It kind of ruins the glamour of the whole thing, and you'll see things you wish you hadn't. The fall is Whistler's "taint," a doldrums lasting roughly from Canadian Thanksgiving to American Thanksgiving.

The first signal that fall is approaching: the luxury hotels in the village break out their Locals Appreciation Romance Getaway Packages. A Village Vista or Mountain Panorama view with breakfast, turndown service and 10 per cent off a pedicure... all for $99! Fall visitors get massive discounts on rooms that rent for up to five times as much during months one actually wants to be in Whistler.

If you find torrential rain and battleship grey at all comforting—and don't mind sharing the breakfast buffet with the regional sales force of a company "taking it to the next level" in Tantalus Conference Room B—a fall Whistler weekend could be just the inexpensive getaway you've been looking for.

You might even luck out and wake up to a clear, crisp fall day, when Whistler is magnificent. Bundling up against the chill, arm-in-arm with that special someone, there is nothing like crunching across frosted maple leaves, seeing your breath in the air and looking up at the first fresh dusting of snow on the peaks.

Just be sure to request a room on a floor that isn't under renovation for the upcoming ski season.

Answer and Question

The victors get to write history, and the sanitized official version would prefer Whistler skip from its origins as a remote fishing camp founded by pioneer Myrtle Philip to the grand Olympic vision of Franz Wilhelmsen, then fast-forward through the seventies and eighties to the vast and efficient recreational theme park that Whistler–Blackcomb is today. Even trolling through the Whistler Museum and Archives, you get the message it would be better if everyone could just skip over the twenty years from 1975 to 1995. Better to forget there were once wet T-shirt contests, squatters and real ski bums in our indiscreet youth.

There was a local newspaper that covered that whole period: the *Whistler Answer.* The *Answer* went into hibernation and reappeared in different iterations off and on throughout those years, but the one constant was its editor and publisher, Charlie Doyle.

The inheritor of the *Answer*'s local voice is the *Pique,* a weekly paper distributed free throughout the valley, but that's a bit like saying the *Georgia Straight* is still the voice of the Vancouver hippie movement. Still, at least the *Pique* takes a stand on community issues and local politics and doesn't just reprint Whistler–Blackcomb press releases—that job falls to Whistler's "paper of record," the *Whistler Question.*

The *Answer* was the authentic voice of Whistler, as post-hippie ski bum as it was do-it-yourself punk rock. Its editorial position was clear from its motto: "For Those Tired of Questions." One infamous *Answer* cover was a close-up photo of a marijuana plant, with the new public safety building and RCMP headquarters in the near background.

Localman originally appeared in the *Whistler Answer* in the late 1970s and early 1980s. He is actually a deformed "Vuarnutian," a native of the lost planet Vuarnet, sent here by his parents as a baby to live among his own kind: the peaceful ski bums of early Whistler. Localman left Whistler to attend Bob Marley's funeral and eventually settled in Vancouver.

WE FOLLOW RAINBOW AS HE ATTEMPTS TO TRANSCEND *PEDAGOGICAL INFORMATION TRANSMITTAL*, AND STRIVES TO *ELEVATE* THE BASIC SCHOOL PROGRAM LESSON TO A MUTUALLY BENEFICIAL, CO-EDUCATIONAL EXPERIENCE.

HAVE THESE *TWENTY ONE* STUDENTS BACK BY NOON, OR THEY ARE IN VIOLATION OF THEIR PAROLE.

I HAVE *NO* OTHER INSTRUCTORS AVAILABLE, SO YOU'LL HAVE TO DEAL WITH ANY *SPLITS* YOURSELF.

A *SPLIT!?* DON'T KNOW THE MEANING OF THE WORD.

CLASS CARD

M. BRAQUAGE

LEVEL 5

JOHN

DO WE *HAVE* TO TAKE LESSONS? CAN WE JUST *GO?* WHAT TIME DOES THE LESSON *END?*

FUN, FUN, *FUN!*

UP THE LIFT...

68

AH, MY YOUNG PROTEGES ARE *ENHANCING* THE EDUCATIONAL EXPERIENCE.

YEAH, EH? WISH I WAS ON *THAT* CHAIR INSTEAD OF *THIS* ONE.

THE PURPOSE OF A DEMONSTRATION IS TO GIVE THE STUDENTS A VISUAL IMAGE OF THE MANEUVER TO BE ATTEMPTED...

THE TURN UTILIZES THE TERRAIN, AND AS A RESULT, IS ROUND AND CONTROLLED...

HEY! A FUCKIN' SQUIRREL! RIGHT ON! GET 'EM!

89 MINUTES AND 32 SECONDS LATER...

NO... *THANK YOU.* THAT'S OUR TIME FOR TODAY. WHEN NEXT YOU FALL, REMEMBER THIS IS BECAUSE YOUR *CENTRE OF MASS* HAS BEEN DISPLACED OUTSIDE THE *POLYGON OF SUSTENATION.*

DOES THAT MEAN WE CAN *GO?*

RIGHT ON.

BYE, SIR!

Pineapple Express

The Pineapple Express is a subtropical jet stream that transports warm, moist air from Hawaii up to the West Coast. The Coast Mountains force this warm air upwards, creating dense clouds and a lot of rain: the nasty Pineapple Express that hit in mid-October 2003 dropped over sixteen *inches* of rain on Whistler and Squamish. To the local weatherman, this is known as orographic precipitation. To most skiers and snowboarders it plain sucks, and leads to anguished second guessing about the decision to buy a pass for the coming season.

Once the Pineapple Express settles in, people in Whistler start gathering animals in pairs and the Sea to Sky Highway becomes a PlayStation game where powered-up SUVs dodge rocks, mudslides and oncoming logging trucks.

When the Pineapple Express arrives in January, as it did again in 2005, even the hardest of snowpacks melts like solder under the torch. It turns mountain streams into torrents, and the packed runs break open into bare patches that resemble soiled diapers. With the freezing level in the stratosphere, and eight inches of rain in forty-eight hours, both Whistler and Blackcomb went to "limited operations." That's a marketing euphemism for closing runs and lifts because the skiing is awful. Two words: Kyoto Accord.

The Pineapple Express seems to have this evil villainish habit of zeroing in on special events such as World Cup Downhills. Not to jinx anything here, I'm just saying...

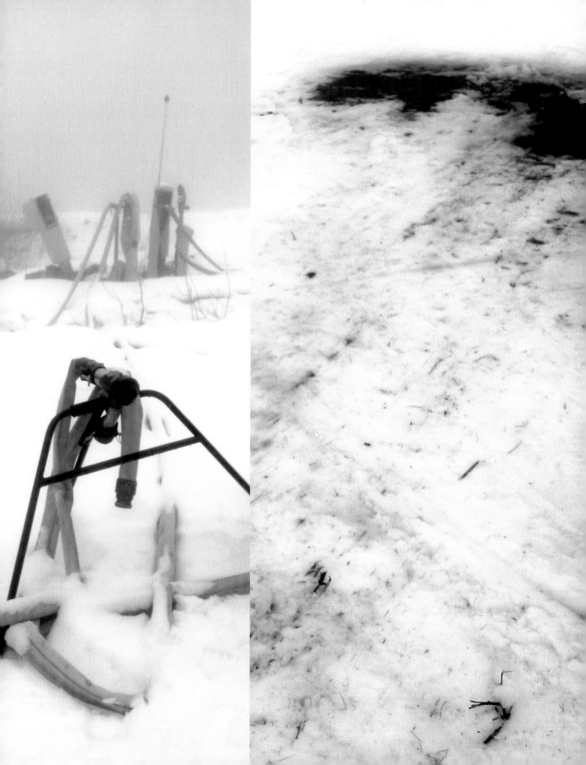

Golf

Golf is a suitable activity for Whistler's "other season" demographic, and the three courses in the valley are world class. Two were designed by golf legends—Arnold Palmer and Jack Nicklaus—and the third by the son of a golf legend, Robert ("Bobby") Jones Jr.

There are other golf courses along the Sea to Sky Highway. North of Whistler, in Pemberton, is the Big Sky Golf and Country Club, designed by the appropriately named Bob Cupp. The course at Furry Creek, between Vancouver and Squamish, boasts a vertical drop that would make ski areas back east jealous. The carts should be equipped with four-wheel drive and winches. Furry Creek is most recognizable as a location for the movie *Happy Gilmore*.

Typically, skiing legends or their children do not design ski areas. Somehow, "Logged by Seppo and some drunken Finns" lacks the cachet of "Designed by Arnold Palmer."

Windsurfing

It wasn't so long ago that windsurfing was Whistler's definitive summer activity. You could practically walk across Alta Lake on other people's boards without getting your feet wet. There's no shortage of "early adopters" here, and a lot of the locals who developed a passion for windsurfing still trek to where the best wind and waves are.

Windsurfing left Whistler behind years ago, and that's cool, because any action sport takes off and evolves where the conditions are right. So unless there are some Dubai-like plans to install wind and wave machines, Whistler will just have to accept that the surf is bigger in Hawaii, the wind is more consistent and intense at Hood River and even the spit at Squamish offers more challenge than the string of lakes that run through the valley.

◆◆ Vuarnets

Nothing defined the look of a late seventies Whistler local more than a pair of Vuarnet sunglasses. For lift operators, ski instructors and cat drivers, your Vuarnets were your talisman; as long as you wore them, nothing could make you leave for a real job. Vuarnet was even the birth planet of Localman, and the sunglasses not only protected his identity but were also the wellspring of the superpowers he once had.

I remember more about buying my first pair of Vuarnets than about buying my first car. I remember hitchhiking to Squamish and back to cash my paycheque from Jim McConkey's Ski School so that I could buy a pair of Vuarnets from Jim McConkey's Ski Shop. Jim sold other sunglasses—he had those rotating white plastic racks of lesser brands like iSki—but Vuarnets were kept under the glass counter, along with other expensive mountaineering exotica such as real Swiss Army knives and Piz Buin.

Vuarnets came packaged in a white box, and printed on the flap in fractured English was the assurance that the lenses had been "Ground with so very hardsand." They cost $60, which to me at the time felt more like $600. I remember the model number—SKILYNX-ACIER VUARNET #4002H—and I remember the salesguy holding them up to the lights in the shop and showing me the tiny "V on skis" etched into each lens. That was their mark of authenticity.

We created new words around our Vuarnets. We called the inevitable knockoffs of their iconic cat-eye shape "Phonets." That sick heartbeat when you thought you'd dropped them or left them somewhere—the reflexive action of reaching for your forehead to see if they were still there—we called that "Vuarnoia."

My Vuarnets remained stylish and functional for years, and I don't remember what finally happened to them. I've spent a fortune on eyewear since, and it is my eyewear karma that the more money I spend on sunglasses, the sooner they will be lost, stolen or damaged. The last pair I bought, from a Wal-Mart outside Kelowna, B.C., cost $19. It's sad, but I'll probably have them forever.

South Side

Many famous resorts have their front side and their backsides, but because of the way Whistler has developed, we've got a south side and a north side—Creekside and Whistler Village. So from an overall presentation standpoint, it's probably come up in Whistler–Blackcomb marketing meetings that it would be ideal if Highway 99 bypassed the south side entirely somewhere past Function, then went up the west side of the valley, turned at the north end of Alta Lake and deposited visitors directly in the village. But that's not the way it is, and the first thing you see when you arrive in Whistler is its backside—the south side, or what is officially called Creekside.

The south side is where Whistler originally started. The old gondola barn was near where Dusty's pub now stands, and the Valley T-bar ran from about where the Lake Placid Lodge is, a few hundred feet up towards the Khyber. You can still see the scar—if you're driving south on 99 from the Whistler Village, look straight ahead just as you start heading down a gentle hill towards the PetroCan gas station and you'll notice a cut-line in the young evergreens that are rapidly reclaiming that hillside. In a day when people were smaller and the climate was colder, that was going to be the slalom piste for the 1968 Olympic bid. (The actual Valley T-bar was moved to the alpine, which is the correct answer to the question, Why are there two parallel T-bars running up Glacier Bowl?)

Most people skiing out at the end of a day at Whistler head down the maze of trails that fan out from the bottom of Emerald Express and end up in the village. Pre-Blackcomb, Olympic Run, once "the longest ski run in North America," was the only way down the north side, and you ended up in a small parking lot near the town's landfill (now covered over by the Whistler Village), from whence you boarded a shuttle back to the old parking lot and gondola barn. Ironically, if you ski down to the Creekside base today, you can take a bus from there to the new parking lot and Whistler Village.

Don't miss out on the south-side experience. Fisheye, Upper Franz's and then Lower Franz's to the valley is without a doubt one of the best high-speed cruising runs in the world. If you want to feel like a Whistler old-timer, hit that in the morning when it's hardpack corduroy and nobody is on it yet. Or make it the last run of the day and stop for a beer at Dusty's. If you really want people to think you're an old-timer, ask the staff whatever happened to that dead horse.

Above, the gondola in 1969;
right, the original Valley T-Bar.

The Japanese

Nowadays in our monoculture world, nothing remains exotic for too long. In Whistler in the late seventies and early eighties, the Japanese were the exotic culture *du jour,* and Japanese skiers were as ubiquitous as Australian resort staff are today. These were the halcyon years just before the Japanese bubble economy popped and, whether it was actually true or not, the local consensus was that it was cheaper for them to ski and golf here than back home.

The Japanese still come here, but they're a very different crowd. They're younger, almost exclusively snowboarders, and more inclined to sport North American brand clothes and gear than the fluorescent outfits adorned with mangled English phrases that the skiers once wore. The younger Japanese seem to come to Whistler–Blackcomb as couples or in small groups, crashing with friends or staying for the season. They are seeking a more authentic, ski-bum experience than that offered by a guided week-long vacation, a role that skiers from the U.K. seem to be filling now.

It wasn't until I spent the 1989 season in Japan that I began to understand this people's passion for skiing. In a country that is 80 per cent mountainous, it shouldn't be a surprise that there are massive North American–scale ski areas like Shiga Kogen, and that skiing/snowboarding is their highest-participation sport. We grumble about driving the Sea to Sky Highway, but the Japanese travelling to Inawashiro, where I was based, would leave Tokyo late Saturday and drive six or seven hours in their version of the Snake, paying expensive tolls every ten kilometres, to squeeze in a crowded day of skiing before turning around and driving back for work Monday. I have always known what an amazing thing Whistler–Blackcomb is, but seeing it from the other side of the Pacific, there is no way I could ever take it for granted.

Any member who has not paid his fees for the current year by October 31st shall lose membership without further notice.

Un membre qui n'a pas payé sa cotisation pour l'année en cours, au 31 octobre, perd ses droits d'adhésion sans autres avis.

All members must attend a recall course every three years. Failure to do so will result in loss of membership without further notice.

Les membres doivent assister à un stage de rappel tous les trois ans. Faute d'assister à un stage résulte en perte de droits d'adhésion sans avis au préalable.

C. S. I. A.

1979-80

A. M. S. C.

C. S. I. A.

1980-81

A. M. S. C.

-20-

FEB 1 5 1979

GARIBALDI LIFTS LTD.
FORBIDDEN PLATEAU SKI SCHOOL
No. 779 Courtenay, B.C.

FORBIDDEN PLATEAU SKI SCHOOL
Courtenay, B.C.

A Canadian Ski Instructors Alliance passport. Other ski areas would comp a member one guest lift ticket a year. Forbidden Plateau, now long gone, once ran a great downhill called the Kandahar.

Easy Street

If you head down Lorimer Road, near the bottom of the hill you'll pass by an unusually normal neighbourhood by Whistler standards. It's a very different place from the Alpine McMansion developments that spend much of their time empty. One of the streets is named Easy Street, and on Easy Street the houses looked lived in, there's stuff in the front yards and real hockey nets on the road.

It took a lot of hard work by some long-time locals to secure a piece of the town they helped build, before it was priced out of their reach. In 1979, a company was formed to buy District Lot 3862, better known as Tapley's Farm, for somewhere around $800,000. This was then carved up into eighty single-family lots (and some parkland that was given to the Resort Municipality of Whistler). These were originally sold for $30,000 to $40,000, with the intention being that affordable housing would be available on a "continuing basis."

It was deemed that future sales of lots "were to remain affordable by being tied to Vancouver housing price indices." In retrospect, that's like tying the cost of ski equipment to the cost of space shuttles.

Whistler needs more Easy Streets, where people who want to live and work here can do so without pinning their chances to a winning 6/49 ticket. Luckily, some entity called Whistler 2020 is looking out for them: they recently developed a policy that confirms the "need to have a resident population."

**Whistler Locals and Pioneers,
Santa's Reindeer and Snow White's
Seven Dwarfs; In No Particular Order.**

Donner
Rabbit
Franz
Blitzen
Myrtle
Vogler
Cupid
Dopey
Chunky
Happy
McConkey
Rudolph
Bosco
Comet
Mel
Sneezy
Boyd
Dancer
Steerzy
Doyle
Grumpy
Buns
Wong
Vixen
Doc
Bashful
Binty
Jojo
Murray
Rox
Prancer
So
Sleepy
Swilly
Hersch
Dasher
Sailer

● Lost Lake

Whether you arrive by shuttle, by bike or on foot, the first question
that comes to mind as you spy this picturesque lake with its beaches,
barbecue pits and skiing and biking trails is, what is so "lost" here?

Before the arrival of the village and the development of
Blackcomb, Lost Lake was a secluded and relatively inaccessible
local hangout. Recreational opportunities were more inclined to
herbs and reggae than juice boxes and the Wiggles. The nudie dock
was not clothing-optional—clothes were simply not an option.

The woods around the lake were once lost enough to support
a sizable squatters' community, but the municipality, the RCMP
and the fire department burned everyone out of their dwellings in
preparation for building the new Whistler Village. Disney-west might
have gained another attraction in the process, but to the locals, the
lake was truly lost.

◆◆ Stickers

Stickers are tattoos for inanimate objects, and you'll see them everywhere at Whistler. They are generally applied by a demographic much desired by marketers: ultra-active young people who are usually very averse to marketing ploys and branding. Like tattoos, stickers are a means of self-expression, a way of telling others that I use *this* board, ride *this* bike or listen to *this* band, and more importantly, you *don't*.

The brilliance of stickers is that they're cheap to produce, and otherwise cool people will voluntarily slather them over every available square inch of their car or truck, bike or board, and on their skis, windows, signs, benches, doors, even lift towers.

There is one particular item, an appliance found in every home, condo, bar or restaurant in the valley, that offers a kind of "perfect storm" of attraction for stickers. With the exception of stainless steel Sub-Zeros, freshly installed in the alpine McMansions of Blueberry Hill, there's not a refrigerator in Whistler that isn't covered in decals from mountain bike, ski, snowboard, skateboard and clothing manufacturers, not to mention bands from every genre of music from Yes to NOFX.

A fridge door is an expansive blank surface crying out to be covered with something. More importantly, the area in front of the fridge is the centre of the social universe, particularly after a hard day of work, riding or boarding. It is, after all, the gateway through which beer must pass.

I'd love to commission one of those conservationists whose job it is to delicately clean soot and remove layers of varnish from Renaissance paintings. I'd get them to delicately lift layer after layer of stickers from an old fridge door. You would travel back not so much in time as back in seasons, from summer to winter and back some more, regressing through a fossil record of music, beer and action sports marketing.

CHECK THIS OUT—SERIOUSLY
HEADS UP BRO—IF YOU SLAP THIS DUCKET ON YOUR GEAR, IT MEANS THE FAT CATS WHO OWN THIS SHOW ARE TOTALLY OFF THE HOOK
SHOULD YOU BAIL HARSHLY
SERIOUSLY—CHECK THIS SHIT OUT!

Sporting this ticket lets you use all these dope rides and hit the parks and stuff, but it also means if you toast yourself or your gear while doing anything, it's all on you. We're talking about shit you haven't even thought of, but if you bring your weak sauce to your board or your ride—even walking around and stuff—and smack into Mother Nature or another dude, or something some dude made (and we're talking inbounds and out); or if like one of the mountain staff, or any of these weird off-shore corporations and like, anyone who even *knows* someone who works for these corporations, or like delivers papers to their house even (that's cold, so call it "Whistler Blackcomb" from now on), drops the ball and you go down, well, tough shit. You are representin' this ticket, which means Whistler Blackcomb is so off the hook if you bite it or RIP, you got nothing. But if you do lawyer up for some lame reason, it all has to go down here in beautiful BC.

DEAL WITH IT: WHISTLER BLACKCOMB IS COVERED NO MATTER WHAT HAPPENS TO YOU.
WE DIG YOUR MAD SKILLZ, BUT SHOW SOME RESPECT AND LOOK AFTER #1 NO MATTER WHAT YOU'RE UP TO.

Proposed Revised Waiver of Liability for Riders, Snowboarders and Younger Skiers.

Legal Spread Eagle

If you've ever taken the time to actually read the waiver of liability that is printed on the back of your lift ticket (or the fine print you sign to get your season's pass or EDGE card), you probably won't ride a lift again. If you are the kind of person who would read a waiver of liability and be *Shocked!* that skiing, boarding or biking are dangerous activities, maybe you should rethink your choice of recreational opportunities.

To take part, you travel to large mountains swarming with other people of wildly varying abilities. There are avalanches, rocks and trees and, unless you're a tele-throwback, you ride up sitting in chairs suspended high above the ground. With an innovative modification to these same chairs, your bike can now ride up too. This means riders now have access to much of the same terrain as skiers and snowboarders, except the cushion of snow is gone, and they crash on solid rock, logs and gravel.

Modern resort operators are very sophisticated, with deep financing and resources. But the message they are marketing at Whistler–Blackcomb contains a paradox. They offer the comfort and containment of a theme park, with all the thrills and excitement you want. Here's the problem—as a skier, rider or boarder, you're the pilot. At a theme park, you strap yourself in for the ride—you're a passenger. If the ride goes off the rails, that's mechanical error, negligence and fertile ground for lawsuits.

You would think that most people who ride, board or ski would be aware of the risks. Everyone I know who skis and/or rides gets hurt at some point. I consider myself fortunate: knocked out for nine hours; dislocated jaw, shoulder and several fingers; cracked ribs, tailbone and teeth; and surgery on both knees. A broken seat post took a core sample of my thigh muscle, and when you factor in skin cancer and pre-emptive mole excisions, I'm easily over three hundred stitches lifetime. I've never sued anyone, because all of these injuries can be attributed to pilot error, which in no way, and without limitation, should hereafter be construed, considered or otherwise assumed to be an actual legal term.

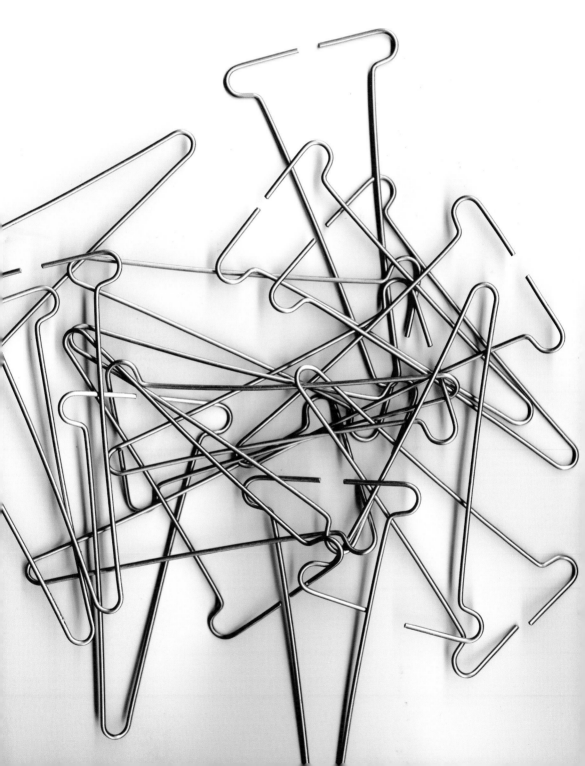

2010

How should we deal with Vancouver 2010? In the parlance of Texas hold'em poker—a "sport" whose broadcasts on ESPN attract an audience that dwarfs NHL hockey, not to mention curling and ski racing—the choice is to either go all in or fold and not go anywhere near it.

So let us all set aside our differences and accept that, for better or worse, the Olympics are coming in 2010. The Winter Olympics—or more correctly, the XXI Olympic Winter Games—will irrevocably change Vancouver, Squamish, Pemberton and, of course, Whistler–Blackcomb. It wasn't that long ago that Vancouver hosted Expo 86, and how that marked the moment the city lost its virginity. We are a little more experienced this time around, and there is no doubt that labour, business and government will do everything in their power to make 2010 a huge success; the stakes are simply too high. But there are elements we can't control, that aren't in our power to change. The obvious one is the weather; despite what the conspiracy websites say, we can't control that, at least not *yet*.

People went to great lengths to point out the perfect conditions at Whistler during the 2006 Winter Olympics in Turin, as if that was proof that the weather would be perfect in 2010. But if the worst should happen and a barrage of Pineapple Express storms pours warm, tropical rain onto the Coast Mountains, there are solutions. The call would go out to every Zamboni and reefer truck driver in British Columbia to gather all the piles of snow that accumulate outside ice rinks across the province and head to Whistler. We would then conscript all the video game testers in Vancouver, which by 2010 should number about 187,000 males under the age of twenty-five. Once they got over the shock of holding hand tools for the first time in their lives, they could set to work spreading the Precious over the Alpine and Nordic venues.

Seriously, the biggest challenge facing Vancouver 2010 cannot be solved by the Vancouver Olympic Committee (VANOC). It is not their responsibility to grab the Olympic rings and drag them into the age of the X-Games, reality TV, TiVo, video iPods, blogging and branded sports entertainment, or force them to compete with the inexorable expansion of NASCAR. Getting all the facilities ready is hard enough. We can't expect VANOC to make the Olympics more relevant.

For the record, I want Vancouver 2010 to succeed wildly, so I'm going all in. In the meantime, let's hope biathlon or curling becomes the Next Big Thing on ESPN (after poker, dominoes and underwater cake-baking, of course). I pray that Whistler–Blackcomb will be happily buried by a three-metre base of snow by early February of 2010, and that a massive, high-pressure ridge of Arctic air will then park itself over the south coast of B.C., bringing clear skies and icy cold for the duration of the Games. And I'd love to see Canadian racers finally win gold in downhill and end up as rich and famous as NASCAR drivers.

◆ Owning the Podium

The International Olympic Committee (IOC) stopped the practice of allowing host countries to put on demonstration sports back in 1992. The original idea was to expose a popular national pastime to a world stage, but when the U.S. put "Monster Trucks" forward as a demonstration sport for the Summer Games in Atlanta, that pretty much did it in.

Not that it's a bad idea: the 1988 Winter Games in Calgary featured three demonstration sports—curling, freestyle skiing and short-track speed skating—that are now official medal events. Canadian athletes seem to benefit from new sports being added to the Winter Olympics. We cleaned up in freestyle skiing in Lillehammer, Norway, in 1994. What happens when the IOC finally lets women ski around with sniper rifles? *Et voilà* , Myriam Bedard wins bronze and two gold. In 1998, at the Nagano games, Whistler local Ross Rebagliati won the very first snowboard medal event.

Looking to Vancouver 2010, the Canadian Olympic Committee has mounted an initiative they call Owning the Podium 2010. It forecasts the number of medals Canada would need to win (35) to be the top nation. It even describes clear strategies for winning more medals and identifies sports in which the most gains can be made. While this atypical Canadian approach to actually *winning* reads like a PowerPoint presentation for Highly Effective People, the goals and objectives are good ones.

A lot of the medal events in a given Winter Games are traditional Nordic events, particularly cross-country skiing, which is dominated by the Scandinavians and Eastern Europeans. In fact, nearly 40 per cent of the medals are Nordic races and relays of various lengths. Given that Canada will likely do well in hockey, curling and short-track (and I hope alpine skiing) if we want to Own the Podium, we either take up cross-country skiing en masse, or we start making up sports.

Proposal for a Demonstration Sport

It turns out that China and the United States, and probably Canada as well, are actively recruiting gymnasts who have *never skied* as potential medal hopefuls for the aerial events. I mean no disrespect to the training and effort that goes into being a world-class gymnast, but I'm having a hard time appreciating a sport where adaptive skills and some ski lessons could place someone on a medal podium. Using that same logic, Alpine Canada could take a drag racer, strap him into a pair of downhill skis, send him to ski school for a couple of weeks and then fire him out the start gate of the downhill. That might not get us on the podium, but it would certainly be entertaining.

This line of thinking gives me an idea for a demonstration sport for 2010: what if we combined biathlon and aerials? So instead of racing around a track and then shooting at targets, biathletes armed with tranquilizer guns race around the track, then shoot at the freestyle aerial competitors. It would be a kind of live skeet-shooting event, and would definitely raise the stakes for the aerialists.

I'm still struggling with a name for my new sport; skeetstyle, maybe? I do know that if the Olympics want to stay relevant, it's that kind of out-of-the-box thinking that will help. It might just add another gold in our quest to Own the Podium.

2011

The season after the Winter Olympics, Vancouver–Whistler will wake up with a vicious hangover, either reminiscing about what a great party that was or trying to figure out how to make up with everybody. But 2010 can't be a one-night stand—we're looking for some commitment here. At some point during the 2011 season, you should at least call or something.

◆◆ **2066**

For release on GoogleNet, February 16, 2066:

To mark the 100th anniversary of **Garibaldi's Brohm–Whistler–Blackcomb–Currie at Squamish–Pemberton™**, the **Google–Dubai Corporation™** is pleased to announce the completion of the new **Common Interest Community at Olympic Station™**.

Thanks to **Google–Dubai™ SeismiVent™** technology, the controlled eruptions of our **PakRim™** volcanoes has finally stabilized the average seasonal temperatures at 2020 levels. We can now guarantee a minimum of 20 **NaturaSno™** days per **KoldSeason™** for our ShareholderCitizens to **SkiBoard™** in/out of the new **Common Interest Community at Olympic Station™**. And for our **HotWeeks™** seasonal ShareholderCitizens, we've planted **YouGene™ H2O–2–Go** engineered grasses that wick away water and runoff, and keep our **BykeTraxx™** in optimum condition. It may be warmer and wetter these days, but that shouldn't get in the way of fun!

Google–Dubai™ is also pleased to announce that all the **ActivTerrain™** below the new **Common Interest Community at Olympic Station™** has been completely enclosed in **NaturaSky™** and combined with our 400 hectares of **DiamonGlyde™** simulated snow surface; **Google–Dubai™** has now created the largest climate controlled **SkiBoard™** and **SafeTGravParx™** facility in the incorporated nation of Cascadia [formerly Alaska, British Columbia and Washington—ed]. Not only does the **NaturaSky™** enclosed **ActivTerrain™** restore the available **FusionLift™** vertical to 1,609 metres, it allows ShareholderCitizens an opportunity to finally access the partially restored **Whistler Pioneer Village and Town Centre at Garibaldi's Brohm–Whistler–Blackcomb–Currie at Squamish–Pemberton™**.

It seems shocking by 2066 standards, but even as late as the **40 25 Anniversary,** ShareholderCitizens and ServiceworkPartners lived in relatively close proximity. In fact, prior to the automation of lift hosting, **SkiBoard™** instruction, **ShareholderCare™** [ski patrol—ed.] and the high-speed fusion rail line to New Cathay [Vancouver—ed.], Whistler–Blackcomb ServiceworkPartners actually lived within the **Google–Dubai Presents Sea2Sky Heritage Recreational Perserve™**. The efforts to restore the **Whistler Pioneer Village and Town Centre at Garibaldi's Brohm–Whistler–Blackcomb–Currie at Squamish–Pemberton™** give our ShareholderCitizens a window to a different era, a chance to recall the savage days of Nancy Greene, Rob Boyd and step-in bindings.

Finally, we are very proud to announce **Google–Dubai's the Beach at Brackendale and Garibaldi Highlands™.** For the first time since the massive 9.2 Tofino Event brought down **The Barrier at Black Tusk™**, draining three glacial lakes in a catastrophic debris torrent that deleted the former city of Squamish from **GoogleMaps**, common interest community and commerce return to the area. From great tragedy arises great opportunity, and with the sea level now constant, **Google–Dubai's the Beach at Brackendale and Garibaldi Highlands™** offers preferred ShareholderCitizens a rare opportunity at beachfront living, a mere seven minutes by **CascadeFusionTrain™** to both **Garibaldi's Brohm–Whistler–Blackcomb–Currie at Squamish–Pemberton™** and New Cathay.

Weasel Workers

The unsung heroes of any successful World Cup Downhill are the volunteer course workers. Whistler has its own distinct group of these folks, and they call themselves the Weasel Workers. They take their name from a particularly nasty section of the Dave Murray Downhill, the Weasel, an insanely steep pitch that transitions the course from the Toilet Bowl through mid-station and on to the lower mountain.

Overnight, Whistler–Blackcomb will Zamboni over twelve hundred acres of runs. But a race course is a different animal, and depending on the snow conditions, cat tracks might do more harm than good. At that point, only boots, shovels and back-breaking work can save a race. Come 2010, there won't be much room in the spotlight for the folks that do that work. But if not for the Weasel Workers, 2010 wouldn't happen at all.

The Weasel Workers spend days and weeks putting up safety nets and fencing and setting out hay bales: all the massive infrastructure a World Cup DH demands. But what makes them so special, besides their dedication, is hard-earned experience and a deep empathy for local snow conditions. It was a Weasel Worker that first brought nitrogen fertilizer (28–0–0) from a farm in Pemberton and pioneered the artificial hardening of saturated soft snow. Weasel Workers are magicians, consistently turning a particularly nasty and temperamental piece of mountain into an exciting and world-infamous race track on par with Kitzbuhel's *Hannenkahm*.

Any group of good guys and gals has to have a nemesis, and for the Weasel Workers, this would be the Fédération Internationale de Ski (FIS), the governing body of ski racing, freestyle and snowboarding. FIS delegates are responsible for athletes' safety and for making sure that races are run according to the federation's standards and rules. In a perfect world, they would be completely impartial and objective, but people like that are only found on *Star Trek.*

In 1980, Whistler was set to host one of the very first downhills ever to be held outside of Europe. The Pineapple Express was hitting the mountain hard. Everyone was pitching in to truck in, shovel and boot-pack snow. Le Cirque Blanc was coming to Whistler and, dammit, we'd be ready. Mother Nature finally capitulated to the sheer effort of the Weasel Workers; the weather cleared, temperatures dropped and the course hardened. We were sure the Crazy Canucks—Dave Murray, Dave Irwin, Ken Read and Steve Podborski—were going to get a chance to dominate on their home turf.

But it was not to be. The FIS delegates, who until then had only been concerned with how soft the track was, started making noises about it being *too fast*. It smelled like Euro-politics from up on the Weasel, and hearts were broken when they cancelled the race, ostensibly for safety reasons. Wengen runs under a railway bridge, and San Moritz and other European downhills seem to go ahead on courses that are more cow pasture than race course. So we all knew the real reason—they were afraid of the Crazy Canucks!

At that point, Ken Read did something that elevated his handsome and articulate self to Patron Saint of Weasel Workers (God of Weasel Workers is filled by Dave Murray, of course). In one of the greatest nose-thumbing gestures in winter sports history, Read ran the course anyway, and without his helmet. Unsafe our Canadian ass—take that FIS!

The Crazy Canucks, left to right: head coach John Ritchie, Ken Read, Dave Murray, Dave Irwin, Steve Podborski, assistant coach Heinz Kapler.

● Sea to Sky

Whether you live in Vancouver or come to visit Whistler from somewhere else, unless you travel the Duffey Lake Road, you will have to drive (or be driven) up Highway 99—the Sea to Sky Highway. The 110 kilometres from Horseshoe Bay to the Husky Station have a fearsome reputation, and even after a $600 million makeover, that reputation remains well deserved.

It's amazing how a city the size of Vancouver simply disappears from the rearview mirror once you exit Highway 1 near Horseshoe Bay and start heading north on 99. It is difficult to think of another metropolis whose sprawl is so clearly constrained by geography, especially ocean and mountain. One moment you're driving through the plush suburb of West Vancouver, the next you're a stunt driver in a spectacular car commercial.

The Sea to Sky Highway winds its way through some of the most amazing and active geological terrain on the planet. But we frequent Vancouver–Whistler drivers have become completely desensitized to the stunning vistas. I'm as bad as anyone, more focussed on anticipating the next passing lane than slowing down or stopping to take it all in. For us, the journey is *not* the destination.

Now, the next time you load up with groceries and wheel out of Someplace Special (as Safeway is required to call itself in Caulfeild) fully provisioned to join the Snake for the drive to Whistler, you'll be able to regale your passengers with some interesting factoids about the places you'll zip past on the way:

Horseshoe Bay

You can call it a village, but in reality Horseshoe Bay is not much more than West Vancouver's begrudged contribution to the Trans-Canada Highway system. It may well have been an idyllic cove once upon a time, but now it's dominated by the terminal for one of the busiest ferry systems in the world. One optimistic tourist website states, "Ferries glide in and out of Horseshoe Bay, and the wake from the larger boats creates surf as they hit the shoreline." Not quite as prosaic as the signs around the naval air station at Whidbey Island, Washington: "Pardon our noise, but it's the sound of Freedom."

The bay was called *cha'xhai* (chai-hai) by the Squamish First Nation, after the swishing sounds made by the masses of schooling fish that found shelter there. Not sure what the Skwxwu7mesh-ulh word for the sound of squishing yachts is, but in the summer of 2005 one of the big superferries threw a gear and used the neighbouring marina for a runaway lane.

Lions Bay

If you look at Lions Bay on Google Earth, you can see that much of the village is built on what geologists call an alluvial fan. This is a radiating sediment deposit, compliments of fast-moving Harvey Creek, which is doing its part to help the Coast Mountains find their angle of repose. After a fatal rockslide in

the early 1980s, massive engineering projects above Lions Bay reduced the risk somewhat. Now that the highway gets commuters to downtown Vancouver in twenty minutes, Lions Bay is a growing bedroom community, and you'll see many expensive new homes clinging to the steep slope. The views out over Howe Sound are incredible; I'm just not sure if I'd get any sleep.

Brunswick Beach

Brunswick is arguably the coldest and most spectacular "clothing optional" beach in the world. As palatial oceanfront estates sprout all around it, access is getting tougher and the locals are becoming less appreciative of one's right to naked self-expression. To say so would be provincial, however, so instead they enforce parking regulations with the veracity of a pit bull. Sun worshippers, you've been warned.

Porteau Cove

A unique combination of campground, gravel pit and world-class scuba diving park, Porteau Cove is also notable for an expensive-looking new pier you hope never gets used. It's a beautiful spot, but the campsites are bone-rattling close

to the railway, as if Snidely Whiplash had planned the place. (By the way, the pier is an emergency facility for BC Ferries, ironic considering the main feature of the scuba park is a number of deliberately sunken ships.)

Furry Creek

Furry Creek was previously only known for a long passing lane and a gated dirt road that left 99 and headed up into the mountains. We rode up there on our mountain bikes once, snuck around a guard living in a trailer and, hours later, found ourselves back at Cleveland Dam in North Vancouver. A few years after that ride, a spectacular and expensive golf course suddenly appeared here.

Britannia Beach

To think that Britannia Beach was once the largest copper mine in the British Empire. After that, for a while it was the home of the World's Largest Truck Tire. You still drive by the tire, but there are bigger ones now somewhere else.

Browning Lake

At one point, Browning Lake had the weirdest fishing regulations ever: you had to be under 16 or over 65 to fish there. The lake is stocked with rainbow trout every year, but if you leave it too late in the season, all you'll catch is a wayward cooler or someone on an air mattress.

Squamish

One can't help think that a town as spectacularly situated as Squamish is only a prestigious film or theatre festival away from becoming the most expensive and sought-after real estate on the planet. By car, it's forty-five minutes north of downtown Vancouver and thirty minutes south of Whistler. It sits astride the Squamish River, on a verdant flood plain in the morning shadow of a 600-metre sheer granite wall, the Stawamus Chief monolith. As a backdrop, there's Mount Garibaldi, part of the chain of volcanoes that run from Mount Shasta through Mounts St. Helens, Rainier and Baker. If that's not enough natural spectacle, Squamish marks the end of Howe Sound, the southern-most fjord in North America. And you know you're almost there when the 335-metre-high Shannon Falls appear on your right.

Squamish was our base camp when we lived at Whistler because there was a supermarket and a Bank of Montreal there. There was no bank in

Whistler, so every second Friday after quitting time, Highway 99 would fill with southbound Whistler locals racing to get to the BMO before closing to cash their paycheques. We'd buy groceries, then high-tail it back to Whistler. Squamish was not a nice place in those days. It took guts to go into the Chieftain for a pint, where the clientele was native, logger, miner or some unpredictable combination of all three.

Squamish today is the poster community for economic diversity. With some of the best rock climbing in the world, great windsurfing at the Spit, killer mountain-bike riding and the annual appearance of three thousand bald eagles for a necrotic salmon festival, the town is quickly moving from a resource-extraction economy to a tourist-extraction economy. By all means, stop in Squamish. There's a Starbucks, which means you can order a "grande half hazelnut decaf soy latte" and no one will mock you. But just don't get too comfortable—that fully loaded logging truck bearing down on you has a bumper sticker that says, "Think fast, hippie."

Brackendale

The road to Whistler once ran through Brackendale, but to the relief of the residents—especially the thousands of bald eagles that come here from

November through January—the highway now bypasses the town and heads straight towards Alice Lake. The chamber of commerce still hopes you'll turn off the highway sometime and patronize the local artisan shop, theatre and native galleries.

Brohm Ridge

In the early 1970s, an attempt was made to build another major ski area in the Sea to Sky corridor at Brohm Ridge. The line of gondola towers that could once be seen climbing over the ridge has since been dismantled, and the huge and expensive alpine lodge is now a haven for snowmobilers and mountaineers; I imagine them living a snowy, two-stroke version of *Mad Max* up there. Stay tuned, though, as the ski area proposal lives again, this time as "Garibaldi at Squamish."

Garibaldi

After you leave the Cheakamus Canyon section of the road, you'll see a blocked-off stretch of two-lane road heading off to the west. That once led to Garibaldi, a town that was never "once thriving," but was certainly better off then than it is now. There were some nice old homes in there, but in the seventies the provincial government realized that Garibaldi Lake might be one big earthquake away from bursting through the Barrier, a massive lava cliff near Black Tusk. So they closed the town before it got washed away, and let those who wanted to, resettle at Pinewood Estates, a moss-covered lava flow.

Brandywine Falls

This picturesque name comes from a bet between two drunken railway surveyors: my bottle of brandy against your bottle of wine that I can guess the exact height of the falls (correct answer: 60 metres). If Brandywine Falls were back east, by now

it would be a legendary tourist attraction, surrounded by honeymoon hotels. As it is, it suffers (or benefits, depending on your point of view) from being on the home stretch of the drive to Whistler, so no one ever stops there.

Function Junction

As you cross the second set of railway tracks, Function Junction is to your left, just before officially entering the Resort Municipality of Whistler. "Function" is Whistler's unglamorous sibling, the one who took all shop electives in school. If you need practical things like a used car or a faucet, Function is the place to go. Here in Function, the sandblasted artisan signs ubiquitous to the village are non-existent; it's oddly reassuring that somewhere in Whistler are businesses that announce with hand-painted signs: WE WON'T BE UNDERSOLD!

If you live in Whistler, you can't get along without Function. But it's not the first impression the planners of the New Whistler would like visitors to have. One day, when they have *Sim City*–like powers, they will probably pick Function Junction up and drop it as far north of the village as they can.

Pemberton
It's fine. Many Whistlerites have fled there so they could buy a home. Let's leave them alone.

The Snake

On any given Friday evening, but especially during the winter, the Sea to Sky Highway is bumper-to-bumper with Whistler-bound SUVs. Predictably, on Sunday evening, the Sea to Sky Highway is bumper-to-bumper with Vancouver-bound SUVs. This *Starlight Express* of Range Rovers and XC90s is known as "the Snake," an entity held together by nothing more than the urgency of folks seeking to maximize their every available weekend moment. You will also experience the Snake early in the morning on pow days, and the construction work on the highway is certainly doing its part, creating a whole series of mini-snakes each time a flag person holds things up for some blasting or rock scaling.

The head of the Snake is usually a car sporting Washington or Alberta licence plates: "beginner plates" to veteran Whistler drivers. The rest of the Snake is made up of Vancouver second-home owners, for example, a stockbroker, his lululemon-clad life partner and their 1.3 kids. There will be the odd local in the mix, easily spotted

because the bikes and/or skis on the roof rack are worth more than the vehicle carrying them.

A new addition to the better class of vehicles in the Snake is the on-board DVD player. When things bunch up, you can see the SUV in front radiating that surreal blue TV glow that flickers from otherwise dark apartments in Vancouver's West End. The legalities of tailgating aside, it's fun to get close enough to see what movie is playing in the car in front.

One mistake that rookie Sea to Sky drivers make is over-reacting to the glare of a million halogen candlepower in their rearview mirrors. The curves can be daunting, but the straight sections are not the place to compensate by speeding up. Nothing infuriates a Sea to Sky vet more than slogging behind a slow car, only to see it accelerate in places where it could be passed.

Mountain Biking

It's exciting to be in on the ground floor of a new sport, and Whistler experienced the explosion and evolution of both mountain biking and windsurfing firsthand. Windsurfing left Whistler behind long ago for bigger waves and higher winds elsewhere. But for a variety of reasons, Whistler and Vancouver's North Shore have been the settings for a revolution in mountain biking, and many (if not most) of the world's best riders and bikes are from here. In many respects, Whistler is now as famous for its mountain biking as for its skiing and snowboarding.

It's barely twenty years since Tom Ritchey's handmade frames made their way north from Marin County to Vancouver bike shops and into the hands of winter sports enthusiasts looking for a summer equivalent to downhill skiing. The Whistler area has a boundless network of logging roads and steep, single-track trails, not to mention a bunch of ski lifts that basically sit idle and don't generate revenue for half the year. And so an incredible action sports feedback loop developed: as mountain bikers got better and went after more challenging terrain, bike technology followed suit, which in turn enabled riders to take their skills to a whole new level.

What really changed the game was the realization that trucks or chairlifts could be used to carry bikes up the hill. This was as important psychologically as it was technologically, as revolutionary as fixing the heel to the ski. Take climbing out of the equation, and it's a whole new sport. When you don't have to pedal up the mountain, the weight of your bike is no longer an issue. You can make the frame super-beefy, equip it with hydraulic disc brakes and cushion the ride with front and rear suspension. In that respect, many world-famous locally designed bikes, such as Rocky Mountain, Kona, Banshee, Brodie and Norco, are basically motocross bikes with their engines removed. And every self-respecting rider now wears a full-face helmet and a complete set of body armour. On first glance, you can't tell a modern mountain biker from their motocross counterpart, except for the value of the sponsorships. Much as you appreciate the support of your local bike shop, they're no Mountain Dew.

The final ingredient in this unique action-sports equation is simple mileage: where riders once spent hours climbing for a few thrilling minutes descending, the ratio has now been completely reversed. In a single day at the Whistler bike park, you can ride more downhill vertical than you could in an old school month. This has ramped up skill levels exponentially, but also increased the carnage rate. Coming down hard on rocks and gravel hurts a lot more than dropping into two feet of pow, and the Whistler clinic does a brisker trade patching up bikers in the summer than it does skiers or boarders in the winter.

But don't let that deter. There really is no better place to try lift-serviced mountain biking than the Whistler bike park. You can rent a full-suspension bike, a full-face helmet and armour up. Absolutely take a lesson, and get a tour from an experienced rider. It'll be something you'll never forget. Just like riding a bike.

■ Music

Music can define an age or a place, and Whistler is no different. The PowerPoint presentation of the Relationship Between Music and Whistler would look something like:

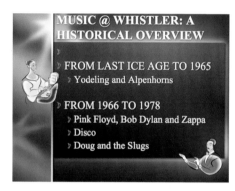

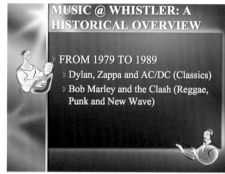

There's never been a shortage of dance floors or venues at Whistler, with or without brass poles. Off the hill, the vibrant live music scene has grown with Whistler's stature, as has the star power of some of the acts to play here. There is a chance the snowboarder you are riding up the Express with is one of the Beastie Boys, and Seal did marry a supermodel here after all.

On the hill, music is more and more a part of the landscape, especially during events like freestyle and snowboard contests. Skiers were quick to adopt the Sony Walkman, that revolutionary portable cassette player, and the iPod has followed suit. As a soundtrack for riding lifts or hiking into the backcountry, music can make the ascent disappear, and before a race, it can help you relax as you wait for your start number to be called. But when you're actually descending on a crowded slope or in avalanche terrain, being able to hear someone (or something) bearing down on you from behind appeals to the self-preservation instinct. I find it hard to ski with music, as the constant changes in terrain and snow always vary the rhythm of your turns. It's hard enough to keep a beat on a dance floor, let alone with a board or skis on your feet.

● Ski Clothes

If you ski, board or bike on the coast, there will be days when you will get wet—it's just part of an active, outdoor life here. There are perfect days, but if you limit yourself to those, timing them with your ski week or days off, you may never get out of the house.

You won't find much down clothing in the closet of a Whistler–Blackcomb skier, unless it's a vest that can be worn under a waterproof shell. Down is all about *loft*, the airspace that insulates you from the cold. It's the best thing for cold and dry, but it flattens like a tortilla when it's wet, and you might as well be wearing denim at that point. As for jeans, they're water magnets, and by lunchtime you'll be sporting knee-high ice gaiters. The highest concentration of denim clothing can be found around the ski racks outside the lodges, among folks trying to figure out which pair of rental skis are theirs.

Your smart Whistler–Blackcomb skier dresses in layers, and one of those layers usually involves fleece. From the inside out, I'd go with thermal underwear top and bottom, a fleece turtleneck and Gore-Tex outerwear, either lined if it's cold or unlined if it's warm. Bib pants or Farmer Johns are the way to go, but nowadays you'll see your fair share of butt cracks, leather belts and Britney bellies in the terrain parks. Gore-Tex gloves are a must if it's snowing, but try to find some with fleece inserts that you can take out if it gets too warm. Having cold fingers truly sucks.

About the only material that is really waterproof is rubber, but that cuts both ways: water can't get in, but it can't get out either. That's what high-tech fabrics like Gore-Tex are all about; the fabric is dense enough to prevent drops of water from coming in, but porous enough to let water vapour—i.e., sweat—out. It's expensive, and works for the most part, but water still seems to find a way in. Unless you avoid chairlifts altogether, the first place you'll feel it is the butt cheeks. After that, it's the top of the thighs. It can be a bit discouraging to see a super-saturated megaflake land on your thigh, pause for a bit as its frozen core melts, then pass calmly through the most expensive of all outdoor fabrics, designed to prevent that exact thing from happening.

And finally, if being fashionable on the hill is a concern, the worst thing about ski and boarding clothes is their incredibly short fashion half-life. By the time 2010 comes around, wearing camouflage will probably be like boarding or skiing in neon or one-piece suits is today. And it wasn't that long ago that neon ski clothes were *it*. At the very least, if you're not in a position to buy new stuff every season, try to stick with colours that don't have names like "salmon."

◆◆ Skiing is the New Snowboarding

In the latter part of the 1980s, many long-time Whistler skiers migrated en masse to the then-new sport of snowboarding. There were a few reasons for this, one being that snowboards are more fun in concrete powder than 210 cm race skis. But I take particular pleasure in pointing out that both skiing and snowboarding would not be the pastimes they are today if it wasn't for snotty punk rock skateboarders.

Growing bored with skiing was really a just a symptom of a bigger malaise. Even the most dedicated skiers had reached a point where they'd stopped developing their skills, and equipment and technique had stopped evolving as well. As snowboarding and the nineties progressed, skiing was left poling along a long, flat ski-out with totally the wrong wax.

But if snowboarding had been no more than a diversion for disenfranchised skiers, it would quickly have become the Hula Hoop of winter sports. It didn't, and is now as popular as skiing. Urban kids in Vancouver—the skateboard and punk rock crowd—discovered a winter sport they could make their very own. With Cypress, Grouse and Seymour reachable from Vancouver suburbs in thirty minutes and lit for night skiing until 10 PM, it was simpatico. Bonus: tons of uptight skiers in funny clothes to laugh at.

At the time, skateboard punks couldn't afford fancy ski clothes and wouldn't be caught dead in them anyway. (Ironically, the current generation of "emo" punkers pay top dollar for 1970s vintage Demetre sweaters and brown White Stag nylon ski jackets, and in retrospect, I wish I'd preserved some of my outfits.) But winter sports and dressing like one of the Ramones is a surefire way to get bone-chillingly damp, if not hypothermic. A quick trip to Three Vets or Army and Navy for surplus army helmet liners, camouflage hunting vests and waterproof work gloves didn't just keep the hardcore boarders warm and dry, it also managed a considerable anti-fashion statement in a Descente and Spyder-clad lift line.

While it was all good at Cypress or Mount Baker, these kids were initially as welcome at Whistler as a baby in Business Class. But operations could only ignore this new source of ticket revenue for so long. In recent years, huge chunks of acreage have been given over to half-pipes and terrain parks, and the shifted demographic is plainly visible in the sponsors' banners that wave over these new facilities. The Land Rover and Fiberglass Pink Masters Race Area has been replaced by the Nintendo Terrain Parks and Pipes. This makes perfect sense: it's as hard to imagine snowboarders dropping into the PricewaterhouseCoopers XTreme HalfPipe as it is imagining snowboarders dropping into, well, PricewaterhouseCoopers.

● Gear

Boating and skiing have some things in common, and at Whistler–Blackcomb, you can test whether you are cut out for either of these activities by standing in a cold shower tearing up $100 bills. It's been only a few years since I've actually had to pay for skiing, meaning buying gear and paying for tickets, and damn if this isn't an expensive pastime.

Most hardcore skiers and boarders are not independently wealthy, so working in the industry in some capacity is the best way to support the habit. Depending on the gig, a job can mean a free season's pass, maybe pro and shop deals on equipment. Work to ski, ski to work.

If you ski or board often enough, you might eventually get good enough that a company will give you gear for free. The thinking is, if people see you using their gear, hopefully they will go out and buy more of it. It's a simple value proposition, and anyone who manages to get sponsored should never take it for granted. In fact, I want to take this opportunity to thank M&D, my first sponsors. Thank you, Mom and Dad. Sadly, in a pattern that was destined to repeat itself more than once in my career, I got old and/or hurt, and they dropped me from the program. Bastards.

If you ski or board ninety-plus days a year, you're condensing the equivalent of three Average Person Seasons into one. At that pace, gear wears out. Not just hardware like boots or skis but also toques, goggles, gloves, long johns; it all adds up. Consider socks. They used to be just socks, but now they come in Left and Right socks that claim to help you ski or board better, for forty bucks a pop. Truth be told, *thin* and *dry* are all you need to know about ski socks, and you can get that for a lot less than forty bucks. It's exactly the same with boating: put the word "marine" in front of a litre of teak oil and it's triple the price of the same stuff at the lumberyard.

One of our pre-season rituals was a trip to Watson Gloves, on East Second Avenue in Vancouver. We would clean out their inventory of factory-second deerskin gloves and buy waterproofing for them at Three Vets. With a pair of fleece glove liners, we had both a cold and warm glove solution. For those wet days, we also bought rubber work gloves, which fit over the deerskin gloves: totally waterproof, even after carrying fencing or slalom poles around the hill. Admittedly, they looked pretty weird, but that's better than being cold and wet. And there were performance advantages too: more than one downhill racer competed wearing dishwashing gloves, a very aerodynamic (and completely waterproof) solution.

The last year I was sponsored was 1994. With careful rationing, I made a half-dozen pairs of slalom and GS skis last another ten years. Late in the spring of 2004, skiing Lower Franz's to the valley, I tore the sidewall off my last pair of Elan slalom skis. No choice but to suck it up, and that fall I walked into a retail ski store as a civilian. Talk about sticker shock.

Ski Boots

Because ski boots are constructed out of high-tech plastics, metal and foam, in a creepy way, buying a pair is like buying a tortoise or a parrot for a pet: you are acquiring something that will actually *outlive* you. Here's proof: in the movie *Waterworld*, a futuristic apocalypse in which the Earth's oceans have risen to cover all the land, the Mariner (played by Kevin Costner) surfaces from a dive to the ocean floor clutching in his hands a prize: ski boots.

Ski boots are easily the most fussed over, tweaked and modified part of a skier's hardware. A serious Whistler–Blackcomb skier can drop his or her boot-fitter's name like a starlet props her stylist. I've had more than one season in which I was in boots 120+ days, and a lot of the hardcore skiers here put in that kind of time and more. We spend hours grinding, padding, melting, heating, punching, taping and shimming our boots in an ongoing battle between comfort and performance. We're talking black toenails and bone spurs that make your feet and ankles look like something from Jurassic Park. My old roommate has lost enough toenails over the years to make a necklace out of them (see page 133). And, while I have no scientific understanding of the process, one weird perk of all my years in ski boots: hairless shins.

Two words of sage advice based on countless ski trips over the years: you cannot drive in ski boots, even with an automatic transmission. Just don't. The exquisite transfer of control from foot to ski that is the blessing of perfectly fit ski boots does not transfer to the accelerator and brake pedals of a motor vehicle. And never travel separately from your ski boots. Consider them a carry-on item. Don't throw your equipment bag in another team's van between races, or bury your boots in your check-in bags. You can always rent skis and borrow clothes, but boots are your most personal piece of equipment, and you will never be able to rent or borrow a pair that feels right.

The toenail necklace.

Short Skis Don't Suck Anymore

Until the advent of shaped and parabolic skis, your skiing machismo was measured in centimetres. In less sensitive times, the saying went, "180s for ladies, 210s for men." Local Whistler legend T-shirt Al printed up shirts with a picture of a hand grenade, sporting the phrase "Short Ski Tune-up Kit." Try wearing that through an airport these days.

Before snowboarding and some fairly recent technical breakthroughs in ski manufacturing, your downhill choices were either recreational skis or racing skis, slalom or giant slalom (GS). Recreational skis were broken down into ability level, from forgiving beginner skis to the top-end "doctor-lawyer" skis—softer and more manageable race skis, premium-priced using the same logic that once made unleaded gas more expensive than its regular, lead-*added* counterpart.

Ski length used to be directly related to the capacity to go fast. Longer was more stable at speed, and shorter offered quicker turning and more manoeuvrability. That general rule still holds, but now the math is far more complicated. Skis (and now snowboards) are built specifically for different types of skiing and snow conditions. There is carving radius to think about, and width is literally an added dimension: wide skis offer broader weight distribution, so they plane better in deep snow. For quicker turns on hard pack or corduroy, fat skis are a lot more work from edge to edge, where carving skis excel. On the other hand, carving skis dive like a submarine in deep pow, and turn like one too.

Associating ski length with manhood is as illogical as driving an exotic car because you feel nature shortchanged you in certain areas. So I freely admit that it took me way too long to get with the program. But now that I'm on a pair of 188 cm Volkl doctor-lawyer skis (and seriously considering 178s), it's nice to know that the equation "tools do not equal talent" still holds. New-school skis won't make you better, they're just more efficient and a lot less work. If other body parts have a problem with that, they can talk to the knees.

A SCHEMATIC REPRESENTATION OF THE STUDENT-INSTRUCTOR RELATIONSHIP IN A SKI LESSON OF THE PAST

136

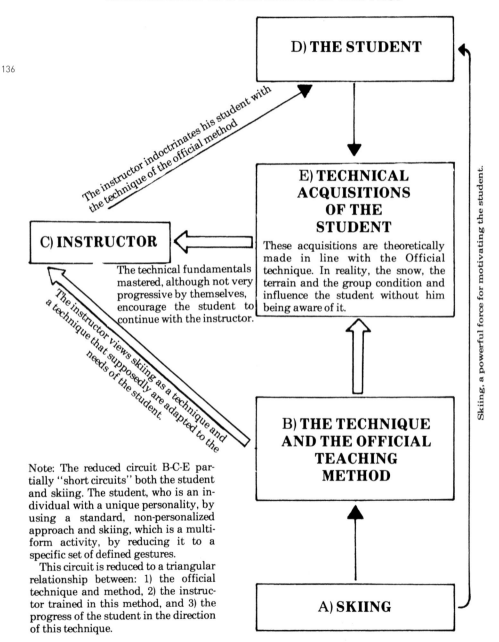

D) THE STUDENT

The instructor indoctrinates his student with the technique of the official method

C) INSTRUCTOR

E) TECHNICAL ACQUISITIONS OF THE STUDENT

These acquisitions are theoretically made in line with the Official technique. In reality, the snow, the terrain and the group condition and influence the student without him being aware of it.

The technical fundamentals mastered, although not very progressive by themselves, encourage the student to continue with the instructor.

The instructor views skiing as a technique that supposedly are adapted to the needs of the student.

Skiing, a powerful force for motivating the student.

B) THE TECHNIQUE AND THE OFFICIAL TEACHING METHOD

A) SKIING

Note: The reduced circuit B-C-E partially "short circuits" both the student and skiing. The student, who is an individual with a unique personality, by using a standard, non-personalized approach and skiing, which is a multiform activity, by reducing it to a specific set of defined gestures.

This circuit is reduced to a triangular relationship between: 1) the official technique and method, 2) the instructor trained in this method, and 3) the progress of the student in the direction of this technique.

240

Top left, Pierre Trudeau and Jim McConkey; above, Wayne Wong—I wish every skier in the world had a chance to take at least one run with him; left, the Whistler Ski School in 1983. I should have suspected it was staff photo day when I discovered I was the only instructor booked for a private lesson at the base of the mountain.

What I Learned From Ski School

First, a disclaimer:

"Someone who wants to learn to ski, or learn to ski better, should take ski lessons from a professional, certified ski instructor."

Why a disclaimer? Because some of the best and worst moments of my entire working life have revolved around teaching people to ski. Absolutely: if you want to learn to ski or board, or want to improve, there is no better way than learning from a pro.

I had formed this romantic ideal around being a ski instructor from looking at my Uncle Wally's *Ski* magazines in the late sixties, and listening to Oscar Brand songs. I knew who Stein Eriksen was, wore reindeer sweaters in high school and understood the progression from snowplow to parallel christie by the time I was twelve years old. Since then, I've worked for four ski schools in my life: Grouse, Whistler, Cypress and a bizarro year at Mount Washington, where I lived an on-snow version of *The Office*. Cypress was amazing because I got to free ski a lot with one of my ski heroes, Wayne Wong. Wayne was one of those people you learned from by just being in his presence.

I lied about my age and passed an instructor's course offered by Grouse Mountain, and got my first ski instructor job when I was barely fifteen years old. I wanted to live and ski in Whistler, but to work for that ski school, you needed to be at least a Level II member of the Canadian Ski Instructors Alliance (CSIA). So in 1977, still in high school, I rode a Greyhound bus to Kimberley, B.C.—an eighteen-hour trip—and at the end of a $300 week-long course and two days of exams, earned my certification. The very next fall I was at Whistler working for Jim McConkey's Whistler Mountain Ski School.

Jim ran a very old-school ski school, before the days of litigation, workers' compensation and the Whistler–Blackcomb playbook. He treated us like professionals, in the golf pro sense of the word. He made us wear white turtlenecks and keep our navy blue uniforms clean, and we did, because Jim said so. He had all our pictures on display, in uniform, in this cedar-shingle frame in his shop. Jim paid us a lot better than lifties and parking lot attendants, and gave us 50 per cent commission on private lessons, which in those days cost sixty bucks an hour. Plus, he'd slip us a chance to go helicopter skiing for twenty bucks when there was a cancellation. Stuff like that just doesn't happen anymore: even lifties used to be able to ski from the top station of a chair to the bottom for a shift change.

The day Jim turned the concession over to the Whistler Mountain Ski Corporation—1982, if memory serves—was a dark one for us ski instructors. Suddenly we were *staff,* and at a surreal orientation meeting in L'Apres, the new management regime laid out how various "job descriptions" had been categorized into "pay ranges." Ski Instructors were now lumped in to the lowest wage category, along with Parking Attendants and Lift Hosts. I believe it was the first time in my life I heard the term "human resources." Things had really changed, and for the first time, I started to feel like it was time to move on.

It is difficult for me not to sound like a retro-grouch in talking about ski schools, and that's why the disclaimer at the start. Even having been in the entertainment industry for over fifteen years, and with the notable exceptions of Jim and Wayne, I have yet to experience more cronyism, politics, brown-nosing and bizarre management practices than I have in the CSIA and in ski schools. I think what made Jim and Wayne unique was their ability to see that my friends and I were insanely passionate about skiing and actually loved to teach.

Back at our old A-frame cabin, we spent many evenings studying classic books like *World Cup Ski Technique* and Georges Joubert's definitive *Skiing: An Art, A Technique.* Joubert's book, long out of print, was practically a physics text. I'll leave you with this: the next time you wipe out, tell your bemused friends your centre of mass went outside your polygon of sustentation. That'll teach them.

● Ullr

Ullr is the Norse god of skiing and archery. That's a bit problematic for marketing folks, because it's not inclusive of snowboarding, mountain biking or extreme interpretive forest walking. There's no Norse god of golf, either, and in terms of "delivering the experience" and "growing the business," Ullr has been underperforming for the Whistler–Blackcomb senior management. Therefore, Ullr has been down-managed to Associate God of Snow at Whistler–Blackcomb, and now reports to the VP, Mountain Operations.

It's not a bad idea to have a little ceremony for Ullr in the fall. All you need to do to stave off the Pineapple Express is to have a glass of schnapps and set fire to that old pair of 210s you couldn't sell at the ski swap. It can't hurt our chances for a good snowfall, and Ullr could use a good review come salary time.

◆ The Boot

Thanks to a real estate developer and the relentless expansion of the Whistler Village footprint, this book was provided some convenient and unfortunate closure. On April 30, 2006, the transition of Whistler from frontier ski town to recreational theme park was officially completed with the gutting of the Boot Pub. This last remaining vestige of authentic local life was given an ignominious and cynical send-off only a PR firm could love: a testimonial Speaker's Corner video, a chance to have your picture taken on the brass pole that was the centrepiece of the Boot Ballet and, to twist the knife a bit, a chance to buy wooden shingles from the rubble for $25 as commemorative collector's items.

The Boot wasn't a West Coast architectural treasure, nor was it built from cedar logs hand-hewn by Myrtle Philip herself. Even the loosest of heritage evaluations would be hard pressed to find an objective reason to preserve the place. The Boot's value is subjective, but that doesn't diminish it. It was the local's living room, a place to have a simple pint after a day of real work. For many of us, it was the first and maybe the last place we got drunk, saw a "ballerina" perform, maybe played a gig. My old punk band played a couple of shows there, and we even set fire to a snowboard on stage, in homage to Jimi Hendrix. Even when the lighter fluid burned away and the p-tex base started blazing, the bartenders didn't flinch. It was the last place left in Whistler to go after a hard day of carrying drywall, or to see bands play for cheap. The late Doug of the Slugs is pogo-ing in his grave.

At the end of the day, no tourist or second homeowner in Whistler is going to miss the Boot. But its closure says something to a big chunk of Whistler locals: it's a signal that what they want doesn't matter. For me, it's the end of a book, and a fitting coda to my younger years living in Whistler.